T0048340

What is
Digital Sociology?

What is Sociology? Series

Elisabeth S. Clemens, *What is Political Sociology?*
Hank Johnston, *What is a Social Movement?*
Neil Selwyn, *What is Digital Sociology?*
Richard Lachmann, *What is Historical Sociology?*

What is Digital Sociology?

NEIL SELWYN

polity

First published in 2019 by Polity Press

Polity Press
65 Bridge Street
Cambridge CB2 1UR, UK

Polity Press
101 Station Landing
Suite 300
Medford, MA 02155, USA

ISBN-13: 978-1-5095-2710-6
ISBN-13: 978-1-5095-2711-3 (pb)

A catalogue record for this book is available from the British Library.

Library of Congress Cataloging-in-Publication Data

Names: Selwyn, Neil, author.
Title: What is digital sociology? / Neil Selwyn.
Description: Cambridge, UK ; Medford, MA : Polity Press, 2018. |
    Includes bibliographical references and index.
Identifiers: LCCN 2018025187 (print) | LCCN 2018027027 (ebook) |
    ISBN 9781509527144 (Epub) | ISBN 9781509527106 (hardback) |
    ISBN 9781509527113 (pbk.)
Subjects: LCSH: Sociology. | Information technology–Social aspects.
Classification: LCC HM585 (ebook) | LCC HM585 .S458 2018 (print) |
    DDC 301–dc23
LC record available at https://lccn.loc.gov/2018025187

Typeset in 10.5 on 12 pt Sabon by Toppan Best-set Premedia Limited
Printed and bound in the United Kingdom by Clays Ltd, Elcograph S.p.A.

For further information on Polity, visit our website: politybooks.com

Contents

Preface   vi

Acknowledgments   x

1 Digital Sociology: Promises and Precedents   1

2 Digital Sociology: Central Concerns, Concepts
   and Questions   22

3 Digital Sociology in Action: Digital Labor
   and Digital Race   46

4 Digital Methods and Methodology   71

5 Being a Digital Sociologist   92

References   115

Index   132

Preface

A print-based publication might seem a rather old-fashioned means of addressing the question of digital sociology. Indeed, tackling any question these days is increasingly unlikely to involve consulting a book. Instead most people's immediate approach to making sense of the question "What is Digital Sociology?" is likely to involve turning to Google (or perhaps Baidu, Yandex, DuckDuckGo and other alternative search engines). Some individuals looking for a deeper dive might check Wikipedia or perhaps search a bibliographic database for a couple of algorithmically recommended articles. In contrast, sitting down and methodically working your way through a 40,000-word book might appear a rather long-winded way of going about things.

This abundance of online information reflects the fast-changing nature of scholarship and knowledge. It also flags up the need for sociologists to pay serious attention to "the digital." Google, Wikipedia and similar information sources are not simply washing over academic disciplines such as sociology and leaving things unchanged. Instead, these technologies are significantly influencing the ways that knowledge is being developed and disseminated. As such, they are technologies that sociologists need not only to be making clever use of but also developing critical stances toward.

From this perspective, there is good reason to engage in "long-form" reading and writing around the question of digital sociology. While the internet is proving a flourishing forum for all manner of sociological conversations, it is telling that a specific sense of "digital sociology" has been most rigorously refined to date through full-length books. Sociological thinking around these issues was first captured in a prescient collection edited by Kate Orton-Johnson and Nick Prior (2013) – fifteen chapters that continue to provide a strong theoretical basis for anyone working in the field. Three years later, this was complemented by a wide-ranging survey of empirical and conceptual pieces edited by Jessie Daniels and her colleagues (2016), showcasing the diversity of "first-wave" digital sociology thinking and research across North America, Europe and Australasia. Published around the same time as these edited collections were sole-authored titles by Deborah Lupton (2014) and Noortje Marres (2017). Among other things, Lupton's book developed a great framework for making sense of digital sociology in terms of digital theory-building, digital methods and digital scholarship. Extending these themes, Marres provided a thorough grounding in the ontological and epistemological challenges thrown up by digital methods of social inquiry and analysis. These four books continue to be must-read references for anyone looking to venture into this area.

As these previous titles demonstrate, long-form books offer a welcome opportunity to slow down and take stock of what are rapidly evolving ideas. There is clear merit in continuing to blog, tweet, podcast and (un)conference about matters relating to digital sociology. Yet there is also clear benefit in engaging in uninterrupted, linear reflection that takes a little more effort and time. So this book seeks to provide a further opportunity to consider what it means to engage in sociological work that "relates to the digital ... is directed at the digital ... but also of the digital" (Carrigan 2015). There are a number of themes and principles underpinning our discussions. On the one hand is an awareness of what is taking place *outside* of sociology. It is important to remember that recent developments in digital sociology have not occurred in a vacuum. In this sense, care needs be taken in locating these ideas in relation to developments beyond the discipline. Indeed, one of the challenges when attempting to talk about digital sociology is the increasingly blurred distinction between straight-ahead sociological work and the mass of cognate work taking place across the digital humanities, new media studies, communications, design and computational subjects. As will be reiterated throughout this book, digital sociology is an inherently interdisciplinary endeavor that spans many different disciplinary boundaries.

On the other hand is the need to remember that this remains a book specifically about sociology. While reflecting on inter/intra-disciplinary cross-overs, we must not forget to emphasize what is inherently sociological about our interests. After all, this is a book concerned with digital sociology rather than "digital social sciences" or "critical digital studies." As such, it takes care to locate current concerns over digital sociology in relation to the "bigger picture" of sociology. One feature of this approach is a willingness to move on quickly from the surface-level features and novelties of the digital. If we are not careful, discussions of digital sociology can soon get bogged down in excessively descriptive and sometimes exoticized stories of how individuals now encounter and experience the digital. Examining the lived experiences of digitally mediated society is important but must be appropriately grounded in what might appear to be relatively dry issues of social structure, political economy, power relations, and so on. Thus while this book considers a range of current hot topics within digital culture and digital life, it does so within appropriately micro *and* macro levels of analysis.

If nothing else, this hopefully gives the book a longer shelf life than many other discussions of digital society. Rather than over-focusing on specific instances of how "the digital" is currently being experienced, this text is concerned primarily with enduring ideas and issues. The arguments, issues and ideas outlined here should remain relevant long after Twitter, Facebook, Mechanical Turk, and so on, have fallen out of fashion. Indeed, there is clear benefit to retaining a strong sense of history when talking about digital society – to remain mindful of where our current concerns sit within the history of sociological thought. In this sense, previous discussions of digital sociology have sometimes suffered from not being sufficiently grounded in the discipline's "pre-digital" work on technology. This book therefore takes care to foreground connections with nineteenth- and twentieth-century sociology – both as a rejoinder to ahistorical accounts of digital sociology *and* as a means of highlighting the strong connections with long-running concerns in mainstream sociology.

So, despite the definitive promise of its title, this short book does not set out to provide the final word on the subject. Instead, I hope that it offers an entry point to a burgeoning field of sociological activity and thought. For instance, there are many writers and theorists whom the book is able only to touch on in passing but are definitely worth engaging with in depth. Chapter 3's overview of digital methods skips through a range of different methods, each of which merits a full book in its own right. Chapter 4's indicative discussions of digital race and digital labor are intended to inspire readers to delve into *other* literatures on equally significant topics. There is plenty more to this area of sociology than can be squeezed into any single title. So I hope that this book will prompt readers to get thinking about the distinctively socio-logical things that still need to be said about the fast-changing "digital" conditions and circumstances in which many of us now live. Most importantly, it is intended to get readers thinking both about what the project of "digital sociology" is and about what it could be. Of course, as with most "What is?" questions in the social sciences, there are few specific straightforward answers to this book's title. Nevertheless, there are plenty of possibilities that warrant our sustained intellectual energy and attention.

Acknowledgments

Given the nature of this topic, much of the intellectual support from which I benefited during the writing of this book came online. I am particularly grateful for the tweets, blog-posts and other forms of digital writing shared by colleagues whom mostly I have never met, from places that mostly I have never been. None of the following people will be aware that they played an important part in the writing of this book, but they certainly deserve to be acknowledged regardless. These include digital scholars such as Karen Gregory, Jessie Daniels, Tressie McMillan Cottom, Frank Pasquale, Trebor Scholz, Mark Carrigan, Mercedes Bunz, Kate Crawford, Melissa Gregg, Nick Couldry, Dave Berry, David Beer, Lori Emerson, Antonio Casilli and the BSA Digital Sociology collective.

Other supportive people with whom I *have* interacted face to face include the likes of Luci Pangrazio, Jeff Brooks, Selena Nemorin, Deborah Lupton and Ben Williamson. Finally, I would like to thank all the staff at Polity for their help in seeing this book over the finish line. The initial idea and commission for the book came from Jonathan Skerrett, with additional editorial support from Karina Jákupsdóttir. Caroline Richmond provided excellent copy-editing and David Watson took care of the proof-reading – reminding me of the continued value of "traditional" publishing in a digital age.

1

Digital Sociology: Promises and Precedents

Introduction

For many people, the prospect of a "digital sociology" might well provoke questions of "why?" rather than "what?" Seasoned sociologists can be forgiven for responding to talk of digital sociology with a weary skepticism. After all, it could be argued that we live in societies blighted by the same basic social issues and problems that have persisted for many decades. From this perspective, it is not obvious why recent technological developments merit a particularly different approach to sociology. Even less jaded observers might be unconvinced of the need for a distinct "digital sociology." After all, surely anyone who is researching, writing and teaching about sociology today is engaged in digital sociology. Aren't all sociologists (at least implicitly) asking questions of digital processes and practices? Isn't everybody now making extensive use of digital technologies throughout their scholarship?

These are understandable reservations to have about a book titled *What is Digital Sociology?*. Yet these five chapters develop an argument that digital sociology is a more serious and substantial endeavor than might first appear. In essence, digital sociology is a call for taking a deliberate and proactive "digital" approach toward *all* aspects of sociological work. This involves writing and researching aspects of social life that are digital in nature as well as form. In turn, this implies questioning the relevance of familiar social methods and theory from "pre-digital" eras, while also striving to develop new ways of inquiring, thinking and knowing. It also means pursuing digitally networked forms of scholarly communication and interaction that are openly accessible, shared and reconfigured.

So, while digital sociology should not be seen as a wholly new (or superior) way of "doing" sociology, neither is it an inconsequential footnote. Despite some appearances to the contrary, digital sociology is not the brainchild of Twitter-obsessed academics who (over)theorize selfies, memes and other facets of internet culture. Instead, it marks a concerted attempt by a broad range of sociologists to engage fully with social settings that are now profoundly digital and digitized. As this book will make clear, realizing such ambitions involves considerably more work than one might think. Indeed, one of the central features of digital sociology is its inherently interdisciplinary nature – pushing sociologists to make connections with other areas that are already engaging critically in digital questions and digital settings. Digital sociology challenges us to take ownership of ideas, methods and techniques that have not traditionally been part of the sociological toolkit.

The sales pitch for digital sociology is therefore straightforward enough – we need a discipline that is fit for the digitally networked societies in which the majority of us now live. This requires sociologists to develop ways of holding to account the digital societies that we currently have, while also constructing plausible alternatives and advocating better futures. Thus the ideas and arguments developed in this book should be seen as enhancing (rather than undermining) established forms of sociology. The idea of a distinct digital sociology is certainly in keeping with sociology's standing as a "living, evolving discipline" (Willis 1996: 107) that looks constantly to question the new. As Dave Beer (2014: ix) suggests, the most productive moments in sociology often occur when the discipline "embraces its uncertainty and turns it to its advantage." When approached in these forward-looking terms, then, there is surely much about "the digital" for sociologists to embrace.

Acknowledging the "digital society"

The case for a digital sociology certainly makes sense if we consider recent technological shifts in how much of the world now interacts and communicates. For example, we live in a world replete with personal digital devices. By 2017, the United States (population of 319 million) had an estimated 223 million smartphone users; worldwide numbers of smartphone users exceed 2 billion. In addition, laptops, tablets and other computing devices are used by a majority of people in developed regions. Crucially, almost all these devices are interconnected and networked. Nearly half of the global population (that is, 3.7 billion people) makes use of the internet – a proportion rising to around 90 per cent of adults in industrialized nations such as South Korea, Australia, Canada and the US (ITU 2017). While it is important to remain mindful of disparities in access and use, being online is an ordinary (rather than extraordinary) element of everyday life.

As a result, most people are now living large proportions of their lives through digital systems, services and applications. Communication with family and friends is increasingly mediated through text and video messaging. Information is commonly gathered through sources such as Wikipedia, social media news feeds, Google search results, online news sources and viral video clips from media organizations. Growing amounts of leisure and entertainment take place online – from the streaming of films and music to mass participation in online gaming and "e-sports." These practices all take place through global online platforms at massive scale. For example, Facebook boasts 2.17 billion monthly active users, followed by YouTube with 1.5 billion and WhatsApp with 1.3 billion (Statistica 2018). Google processes an average 40,000 search queries every second. Wikipedia is now available in over 280 languages, with the English-language version comprising nearly 5.5 million articles.

Such developments reflect the fact that contemporary society is increasingly organized and administered through digital systems, services and applications. Consider how citizens are now likely to engage with education, health, legal and welfare systems. What once were vast paper-bound bureaucracies are now being reconfigured as vast digital bureaucracies. Digital technology is now a key element of the democratic process, as evident in recent national elections around the world. For example, while ballot collections might still rely on paper voting slips, much else of Donald Trump's rise to the US presidency toward the end of 2016 related to social media, email hacking and digital (dis)information. The cumulative consequences of what might seem to be trivial digital practices can surprise even the most tech-savvy observers.

Significantly, these shifts are economic as well as civic and cultural. Contemporary society is shaped by the digital economy. The buying and selling of goods and services increasingly takes place online, and financial trading is now a wholly "virtual" affair. Consumers are engaged in online banking and contactless payments. At the same time, many forms of work and employment are digital in nature (if not form). Amid these developments, the high-tech sector is a dominant part of the global economy. The top three global companies by the beginning of 2018 were all from the technology sector – Apple Inc. (with a market capitalization of $880 billion), Alphabet Inc. ($820 billion) and Microsoft ($725 billion) (Neate 2018). Whereas financial reports in the late twentieth century would celebrate the fortunes of General Motors, Walmart and Exxon, now the talk is of Facebook, Apple, Netflix and Google.

The need for a digital sociology does not stop at these current trends. It is salutary to think beyond the current era of smartphones, apps and websites and toward emerging technological developments. The much anticipated Internet of Things is beginning to take (actual) shape, with network-connected sensors, processors and other electronics being embedded in everyday objects – from refrigerators to clothing. The ability of "smart" objects to collect, receive and process data looks set to alter significantly the relationships that people have with the material environment, as "physical spaces" become overlaid with "code spaces." Indeed, ongoing developments in artificial intelligence (AI) and "Big Data" processing have prompted growing debate over the significance of autonomous systems, algorithmic decision-making and a general blurring of humans and machines. While the precise nature and consequences of these developments remain uncertain, the ongoing digitization of society along such lines is set to continue for the foreseeable future.

Preceding sociologies of technology (a brief history)

If we accept that the digital is a recent development with significant bearing on contemporary society, then there is surely good reason for sociologists to be concerned with how their thinking, practice and craft might better reflect these changes. However, these current concerns need to be properly situated within the long tradition of sociological thought on technology. Before unpacking the ostensibly new turn of digital sociology, it is worth taking time to trace the origins of our current enthusiasms within preceding sociologies of technology. While these thinkers might not have been concerned with "digital" technology per se, there is clearly a lineage that our current discussions need to acknowledge and draw upon. Indeed, it could be argued that digital sociology continues a long history of sociological thought on technology. This can be grouped loosely into three phases of cognate work.

(i) Classical sociologists and technology

Digital sociology does not mark the first time that sociologists have turned attention toward technology. In fact, technology has been a sociological preoccupation since the beginnings of the discipline. Late nineteenth-century sociology emerged in response to economic and societal shifts that were entwined with the development of "new" technologies – not least the emerging industrial era, the rise of capitalism and the shift from religion to science. As such, it is worth remaining mindful of the "vibrant and consistent interest in technology among sociology's forefathers" (Gunderson 2016: 41).

Indeed, many of the early sociological thinkers had something to say about technology (often, more precisely, about "machines"). For example, Auguste Comte's description of phased societal progression was driven by his valorization of a final technocratic "scientific phase." This has prompted claims that Comte's writing from the first half of the nineteenth century "reads very much like elements of a Silicon Valley manifesto" (Quill 2016: 89), with irreconcilable social and political issues reduced to technical problems with technological solutions. In contrast to Comte's conspiratorial "technological optimism" (ibid.: 96) was the writing of Max Weber. While Weber is best known for his work on rationalization and the technocratic "iron cage of bureaucracy," he wrote widely on the development of industrial, military, architectural and musical technologies. For example, Weber was concerned by the reframing of military officers as "technicians" in an era of increasingly modern "mechanized" warfare. His studies on the development and diffusion of musical instruments (such as the piano) prefigured more recent trends to focus on mundane technological artifacts. Unlike Comte, Weber conveyed a deep ambivalence toward these innovations of his time, drawing attention to the compromised social conditions of technological development (Maley 2004).

While technological concerns were apparent in the work of many classical social theorists, the US sociologist Torsten Veblen has perhaps the strongest claim to advancing "a conscious and explicit sociology of technology" (Weinstein 1982: 46). Veblen was the original English translator of key German texts on "*Technik*," thus hastening the adoption among Anglophone writers of his preferred term "technology" rather than the more pointed European notion of "technique" (Morozov 2011). Veblen is credited as the first to challenge the notion of technological determinism – i.e. the commonsense presumption that technology is autonomous and drives history. Instead his work reasoned that institutional and corporate "vested interests" often acted to constrain the development of new technology – making it often more beneficial for institutions (and countries) to engage in forms of technological "borrowing" rather than innovation. As such, Veblen advanced a persuasive account of the social nature of technology development and diffusion. As he reasoned, "the scope of the process is larger than the machine" (Veblen 1904: 5).

Of course, the leading classical social theorist on technology is generally considered to be Karl Marx. The machines of modern industry were a central element of Marx's account of the economic system of capitalism. His work explored the economic *and* social effects of technology – questioning not only the economic impact of machines on prices, cost and production but also the impact that machines had on the social organization of work and workers' lives. Marx's writing on technology remains compelling, and he evocatively described steam-driven "cyclopean" machines operating amid the "giant" of modern industry. He also thoroughly researched the history of technological development, engaging closely with the work of engineers such as Charles Babbage and looking back to the handicraft tools of the Middle Ages and pre-industrialized manufacturing machines such as the handloom. Throughout his writing, Marx refined the idea that technologies are entwined with the social, economic and political conditions of their times.

Marx's thinking gives sociology an enduring legacy of framing technology in a double-edged manner. On the one hand, much of his writing points to the ways in which machines enabled and extenuated conditions of domination and exploitation of workers by capital. He showed how the increased automation of industrialized machines led to an intensification of work, longer working hours, the deterioration of working conditions and the displacement (if not outright dismissal) of workers. As Marcuse (1964) notes, Marx's work is especially perceptive in illustrating how domination is perpetuated *through* technology and *as* technology. On the other hand, Marx also retains a sense of hope that societies might be able to make use of these technologies in alternative, more humane ways. Thus Marx draws attention to the emancipatory potential of technology – writing on occasion that technology offers an opportunity for superseding wage systems and establishing truly social systems of production (Roth 2010). In this sense, Marx laid foundations for an even-handed critique of technology that has persisted throughout many subsequent sociological accounts of technology. As Matthewman (2011: 29) observes, Marx "had an admiration for the things that technology could do and contempt for what it was used to do."

(ii) Twentieth-century sociologists and technology

As sociology grew as a discipline across the twentieth century, so too did sociological accounts of the considerable technological developments of the time. One prominent voice in the first half of the century was William F. Ogburn – a US sociologist whose career returned regularly to questions of technology and change. By early twentieth-century standards, Ogburn was notable for his attention to cultural and societal aspects of technological development. He reasoned, for instance, that technological inventions did not result simply from creative individual genius of "great men." Instead, he described how the development of new technologies "are in large part culturally determined" (Ogburn and Thomas 1937: 91) – a fact demonstrated by the simultaneous emergence of similar technological "breakthroughs" by different "inventors."

Ogburn also explored the repercussions of technology development – proposing the idea of "cultural lag" whereby social life and institutions are seen to adapt more slowly to developments in "material culture" (notably the invention of technology). This lack of societal adjustment therefore resulted in social problems and disorganization. In this way, Ogburn pre-empted later popular ideas of technology "diffusion," "convergence," "innovation" and second-order effects of technological development. While Ogburn's writing could now be said to "read like a parody of technological determinism" (Volti 2004: 399), he nevertheless acknowledged the "complex of interconnections" between social institutions and technology (Ogburn 1936: 2). While limited, Ogburn's work laid the ground for more nuanced discussion of the role that technology plays in shaping aspects of society and culture.

Of course, Ogburn's implicit determinism and presumption of the benefits of technological invention prompted criticism from other sociologists. Around the same time, for example, Lewis Mumford was arguing for more politically nuanced understandings of societal adjustment to technology – often advocating for "change in a direction *opposite* to the machine" ([1934] 2010: 316). Mumford wrote of "technics" rather than technology, evoking the Greek notion of "*techne*" to position technological tools as part of broader social practices. This allowed him to distinguish between two opposing modes of technology. He described "polytechnics" as the combined use of small-scale and versatile tools and practices in ways that were "life-orientated" and concerned with addressing human problems. In contrast, "monotechnics" described the development of "mega machines" that are immensely powerful yet diminish humanity and human interests. For example, Mumford saw the dominance of road networks based around automobiles as leading to unacceptable environmental degradation as well as marginalizing more life-affirming forms of transportation (such as walking, cycling or public transport). As one of his enduring quotations puts it, "forget the damned motor car and build the cities for lovers and friends" (cited in Jackson 2011: 67).

Mumford's concerns over such "megatechnics" pointed to the environmental and ecological consequences of technology. He argued for restraint in order to reach a "dynamic equilibrium" between technological development and ecological, biological and human needs (thus establishing what he termed an "economy of plenitude"). Yet this stark outlook was not without hope. Mumford also argued that humans are defined by the limits of their bodies, minds and human nature – meaning that technology can never be all-defining. Because of this, he reasoned that humans will always retain a consciousness of technology and, with it, a possibility of redefining the role it plays in their lives. As Mumford concluded his 1970 book *The Pentagon of Power*: "for those of us who have thrown off the myth of the machine, the next move is ours."

Alongside sociologists such as Ogburn and Mumford, the twentieth century saw a succession of socially inflected accounts of technology from non-sociologists. In particular, a number of major twentieth-century philosophers addressed technological issues – from Heidegger's *The Question*

Concerning Technology to Lyotard's discussions of knowledge in an era of information-processing machines. One prescient approach is the work of Jacques Ellul. Over the course of seventy years, Ellul constructed an insightful yet bleak account of modern technological society and its diminished human freedoms. Rather than "technology," Ellul wrote of "technique" – i.e. "the totality" of technological artifacts and accompanying processes, practices, rules and institutions. For Ellul, "technique" constituted the system (and systemic logics) within which social life takes place. He reasoned that the emerging technological system of the twentieth century was predicated upon the valorization of efficiency. Thus all technologies are expected to contribute to increased efficiency – "the defining force of a new social order" (Ellul 1964: 17) that privileges characteristics of technical rationality and artificiality at the expense of interests related to "humanity" and "the natural world."

In this sense, Ellul bemoaned what he saw as an increasingly prevalent state of "autonomous technology" where technology becomes an end rather than a means. While the development of any new technology remains a socially influenced and contingent process, it is nevertheless embedded in the underpinning imperative of continued development of ever more efficient techniques. Thus the solution to any societal problem is always understood to be the production of new technology. In his later writing, Ellul (1990) referred to this as "the technological bluff," where people unquestioningly accept technological change as problem-solving and advantageous even when it acts to destroy values, ethics and other aspects of "humanness." Ellul therefore offered a "despair[ing]" (Feenberg 1995) view of the technological society being in constant "dialectic tension with human freedom" (Garrison 2010: 197). Crucially, he saw little hope of this tension being resolved. Ellul reasoned that people are either "fascinated" or "diverted" by technology and therefore have little desire and/or time to be critical. Thus the only ways that this impasse might change would require large-scale destructive war, the unlikely event of "God decid[ing] to intervene," or a sudden large-scale shift in human awareness of "the threat" of technological society (Ellul 1964: xxx).

(iii) STS (science and technology studies)

These early accounts offer useful ideas, although all have clear limitations and gaps when set against the complexities of the contemporary digital age (see, for example, Ritzer 2013). Perhaps the closest twentieth-century precursor to digital sociology is the interdisciplinary field of "science and technology studies" (STS). STS emerged in the 1970s, bringing together a variety of academic areas interested in engaging critically with science, engineering and technology – the history of science, the philosophy of science, anthropology and public policy. Much early STS work drew on theory and method from the sociology of scientific knowledge to address the scientific controversies of the time. Concerns over the Cold War, nuclear power and emerging ecological crises provided early STS scholars with ample subject matter.

Despite its titular "T," STS has a long-standing ambivalence toward technology. Many STS scholars make no distinction between technology and science, preferring to talk in terms of "technoscience," where technology and science are understood as linked and developing in tandem. However, the 1980s saw a burgeoning interest in technology within some areas of STS – prompting pronouncements of a "turn to technology" and what Woolgar (1991: 21) described as "an almost indecent rush by some sociologists of scientific knowledge into the social study of technology." Underpinning this turn was growing recognition of a need to unpack the sociotechnical nature of technology. As Thomas Hughes (1983: 1) put it, this is the idea that "technological affairs contain a rich texture of technical matters, scientific laws, economic principles, political forces, and social concerns." During the 1980s and 1990s, sociologists working in STS set about addressing the ways in which social, political and economic factors influenced the technologies that ended up being developed and implemented in twentieth-century society, paying particular attention to the contested nature of technological design and uptake.

Against this background, STS has long posed a set of probing questions of technology that map onto current concerns of digital sociology. One ongoing issue is the (non-)

neutrality of technology, encapsulated in Langdon Winner's (leading) question "Do artifacts have politics?." Winner (1986) highlighted two ways in which this was indeed the case. On the one hand, he argued that technological artifacts can be designed and implemented (often unconsciously) to have particular social effects. Here he recounted a story of bridges on the Long Island Expressway being designed to be sufficiently low to allow passage for cars but not public buses. On the other hand, he argued that some technological artifacts can be "inherently political" in that they require specific social conditions and political arrangements to operate. Winner illustrated this with the example of nuclear power reactors requiring the existence of a strong centralized, authoritative state.

While influential, Winner's arguments attracted considerable pushback within STS circles. One prominent counterargument was the development of "social construction of technology" (SCOT) by other STS luminaries such as Wiebe Bijker and Trevor Pinch. It has subsequently been contended that "SCOT signals sociology's rediscovery of technology" (Matthewman 2011: 92). At the time, however, the idea of technology as socially constructed was seen simply as a necessary way of contesting technological determinist accounts of technologies having a fixed character, purpose and agency. Instead, SCOT promised a way of "opening up the black box" of technology (Pinch 1998). Key here was the idea of the "interpretive flexibility" of any technological artifact, especially during initial stages of technology design and use. From this perspective, there is no necessary or obvious way that any technological artifact should be designed or used. Indeed, designs and uses will vary between different groups and contexts and often result in conflict between competing views and ideas.

While describing technology as socially constructed, SCOT does not position technologies as permanently devoid of fixed meaning or actions. Instead, SCOT sees the diversity of interpretations of a technology as likely to diminish over time, often until its agreed meaning reaches a stage of "stabilization" and sometimes "closure." An alternative point of view is offered by a third reflexive strand of the STS turn toward technology – the idea of "technology as text." This developed the idea of interpretive flexibility further, challenging the idea that technologies can ever have stable or even "closed" attributes. Instead, as Steve Woolgar (1991) proposed, perhaps there is no "essence" of technology beyond the meanings that people ascribe to it. From this perspective, any technology needs to be understood in terms of its "essential indefiniteness" and indeterminacy.

While they are clearly not in full agreement, some important ideas recur throughout these approaches. First is an adherence to "symmetry" in telling all sides of the story of any technology. This involves recognizing that there is no one script or pathway that a technology will follow. Thus STS places great emphasis on giving equal consideration to dominant *and* peripheral opinions, successful *and* failed versions of the technology. This requires paying attention to all "relevant social groups" (from the most minor influences to the major shapers). Second is a disposition to be contrary and belligerent while also creative and well-humored. Indeed, Gunderson (2016: 46) describes the "aesthetic standard" in STS as including a "playful seriousness, attention to thick descriptions of the mundane, pleasure in subverting common assumptions." Third is an underlying interest in identifying alternatives – particularly in terms of working out how technology might better act in the public interest. A key STS interest lies with "deliberative democracy" – supporting the discussion and debate of significant science and technology controversies that affect wider society. Thus STS looks for ways that marginalized and excluded versions of what a technology could be are given greater prominence through representative means.

Previous "digital sociology" by another name

In terms of historical precedents, it is also worth acknowledging other prominent bodies of literature that precede and underpin the current digital sociology turn. As is evident from the previous sections of this chapter, one of the clear gaps in sociological discussion of technology throughout the most of the twentieth century was a lack of women's voices and critical accounts of gender and technology. Thus second-wave feminism during the 1970s and 1980s prompted the emergence of a "feminist technology studies," reasoning that "technology itself cannot be fully understood without reference to gender" (Cockburn 1992: 32). This work moved quickly from the long-standing question of "women in technology" (more pointedly, the *lack* of women in technology) into critiquing the gendered ways in which dominant twentieth-century technologies were designed, perceived and experienced. Seminal work included studies of domestic and reproductive technologies – problematizing the gendered assumptions underpinning the social and cultural construction of these technologies, practices and relations that surrounded them (see Stanworth 1987). Subsequent work focused on the gendered nature of everyday computer and telecommunications use, alongside the gendered nature of digital technology design, contexts of use, stereotyping and identities of users (see van Zoonen 1992). While disagreements persist over the implications of these analyses (i.e. whether masculinized technologies should be reshaped or rejected outright), such work was key in shifting academic attention away from technological artifacts and toward cultures and practices of use.

Alongside the consistent focus of these analyses on technology's role in reproducing patriarchy, the third wave of feminism during the 1990s was notable in celebrating the radical possibilities for destabilizing conventional gender differences (Wajcman 2009). Key here was Donna Haraway's *A Manifesto for Cyborgs* (1985) – a hugely influential provocation on the social possibilities thrown up by the fast-dissolving boundaries between machines, humans and animals implicated by advances in biotechnology and "cybernetic organisms." Crucially, Haraway describes the cyborg as a politicized entity, subtitling her manifesto "Science, Technology, and Socialist Feminism." This account is intended to subvert meanings surrounding digital technology – putting forward alternative views, language and practices. Haraway's thinking kick-started a subsequent "cyber feminist" literature through the 1990s where writers like Sadie Plant (1996) argued that internet technologies were essentially female (i.e. non-linear, self-replicating systems, weaving connections and multitasking in intuitive ways). Moreover, emerging virtual technologies were seen to provide women with opportunities for developing subjectivities free from embodied gender cues. As Plant (ibid.: 181) contended, "cyberspace is out of man's control." This work takes a provocatively optimistic (if not utopian) view of women assuming control and disrupting technology practices. It is also highly playful and creative – reveling in the uncertainly of cutting-edge technology development and bringing academics together with artists, designers, writers, software developers and activists.

Digital sociology also owes a debt to sociological commentary on the "information society," "knowledge society" and "post-industrial age" that flourished toward the end of the twentieth century. Here, a number of authors attempted to make sense of economic, occupational, spatial and cultural shifts relating to new information technologies – with many proclaiming the emergence of a markedly different era. Perhaps best known is Daniel Bell's description of "post-industrial society." Writing in the early 1970s, Bell explored the sociological implications of an economy predicated upon data processing and the production of ideas and knowledge. Bell's *The Coming of Post-Industrial Society* ([1973] 1999) pointed to the rising prominence of occupations in information work and anticipated the rise of "theoretical knowledge" – i.e. societies run on the basis of abstract models, frameworks and simulations facilitated by "intellectual technologies" (rather than empirical understanding and/or practical intuition).

While Bell was speculating largely on developments in mainframe computing and telecommunications, Manuel Castells's *The Information Age* trilogy in the second half of the 1990s offered an authoritative account of the social structures arising from the increased connectivity of the internet and worldwide web. Castells describes a burgeoning "information capitalism" unfettered by constraints of time and geography. In this sense, the network society is conceptualized as a "space of flows" rather than a "space of places." As is the case with macro-level analyses, such accounts of information-infused societies have obvious limitations. From Bell to Castells, accounts of a new form of information society arising from technological developments have understandably faced accusations of technology determinism. Fifty years after the publication of *The Coming of Post-Industrial Society*, these descriptions remain ideal types rather than accurate reflections of reality for most people around the world. Yet such writing certainly reminds us of the capacity of sociology to address grand economic, political and cultural implications of the digital age.

Finally, digital sociology also has clear affinities with the past twenty-five years of "internet studies." Since the early 1990s, internet studies have brought sociologists together with other disciplines concerned with social aspects of the internet. These include media and communications studies, cultural studies, economics, policy studies, law, psychology, information studies and computer science. Barry Wellman – one of the leading sociological lights in the field – described internet studies originating as a "user studies" off-shoot of the otherwise software-focused field of research into "computer-supported collaborative work." An initial feature of this social turn was internet studies scholars' exploration of "virtual community" and online identity (Turkle 1995; Rheingold 2000). Studies here explored how groups of users formed and interacted through the early listservs and bulletin boards of the 1980s and 1990s and later within "virtual worlds" and on social media. Over the past three decades, internet studies have continued to focus on "how community dynamics continued to operate on the internet ... and how intertwined offline relationships were with online relationships" (Wellman 2004: 125).

Other strands of internet studies have developed to explore issues of internet governance (focusing on areas of policy, law-making and regulation) and internet democracy (covering issues such as the online public sphere, e-democracy and civics). Perhaps the most enduring line of inquiry has been on everyday internet use. This includes studies exploring the use of the internet in domestic, workplace and other organizational contexts, corresponding with other work concerned with detailing patterns of internet non-use – i.e. so-called digital divides, gaps and inequalities (Norris 2001). During the 2000s, internet research burgeoned across media and communications studies, exemplified by the increasingly prominent Association of Internet Researchers led by scholars such as Nancy Baym, Alice Marwick, Kath Albury, Jean

Burgess and many others. Together, these approaches constitute a solid body of sociological work detailing "the rapidly changing dynamics of networked societies and the institutions and individuals within them" (Dutton 2013: 1).

So why "digital sociology" ... right here, right now?

In many ways, then, it could be concluded that there is nothing radically new about the idea of a digital sociology. Sociological questions have been asked of technology throughout the development of the discipline. Thus it is worth acknowledging that sociologists had established a good grasp of social, cultural, political and economic implications of technological change long before the advent of Facebook and Google. Current enthusiasms for digital sociology certainly echo previous sociological "turns" to technology over the past 100 years or so. In this sense our subsequent discussions need to remain mindful of those that have come before.

In particular, the "pre-digital" theorists and researchers just outlined provide digital sociology with a number of useful starting points. There is above all a variety of well-tested questions, existing methods and established approaches for digital sociologists to appropriate. For example, this previous work reminds us of the need to interrogate the transformative claims that are attached to any new technological development, be it optimistic claims of empowerment *and/or* dispirited accusations of disempowerment. From Karl Marx onward, there has been ongoing debate whether technology has essential qualities and characteristics or whether it is socially constructed. Moreover, if technology does not "determine" society, then what exactly is the relationship between social change and technology? These are long-standing questions that digital sociology needs to continue to address.

These previous analyses also provide a ready selection of pertinent issues, problems and areas of inquiry. For example, sociologists from Max Weber onward have been concerned with how technology is entwined with issues of efficiency, rationality, power and control. In particular, this focuses attention on the systems and structures that are associated with the development of new technology. This also foregrounds the importance of the political economy of technology development and implementation – not least associations between technological progress and economic interests and ideologies. Conversely, work in the late twentieth century in feminist and internet studies draws attention to the entwining of technology with issues of identity formation and identity politics. This writing and research highlights the role of technology in the reproduction of inequalities and injustices. Echoing scholars such as Mumford and Ellul, it also points to the likely unintended consequences and hidden costs of technology use – ranging from ecological destruction to the diminishment of humanity and human freedoms.

Some of the work just outlined also demonstrates various approaches that technology scholarship can take, from the cyberfeminist interest in combining activism and art to the STS mindset of being playfully argumentative and belligerent. These precursors therefore suggest that there is little reason why digital sociology should not strive to be creative, transgressive *and* spiky. The fact that "technology" is a topic that lends itself to a degree of speculation and engagement with unknown futures means that digital sociologists have license to be a little off-kilter and playful in what they do and how they do it. This is a topic that lends itself to speculation, provocation and experimentation.

Finally, the body of preceding work also steers digital sociology toward a range of useful dispositions and ambitions. While writers such as Marx, Ellul and Winner were profoundly critical of what they perceived technology to be, they were not devoid of hope. However bleak, much of this previous work consoled itself by considering alternatives and thinking otherwise. Thus current digital sociologists are well advised to keep at least half an eye on "alternative technology," "responsible innovation" and "deliberative democracy." Although tackling what might seem to be all-encompassing conditions such as dataveillance and platform capitalism, digital sociology does not have to result in wholly dystopian, hopeless conclusions.

Current work in digital sociology therefore has much to learn from its heritage in this pre-digital sociology. These are themes that will be referred back to throughout this book. Nevertheless, it is perhaps fitting to conclude this opening chapter by acknowledging the aspects of digital sociology that *are* different, new and distinct from what has gone before. While digital sociologists are standing on the shoulders of giants, we need to be confident in the things that digital sociology can do that Marx, Weber, Ellul and STS do not. From this perspective, there are at least three lines of distinctiveness that spring to mind.

First, digital sociology allows us to make sense of very different technological conditions than those described by previous generations of sociologists. While continuities are apparent, the current wave of digital technologies is quantitatively and qualitatively distinct from the technological conditions that previous generations of sociologists have addressed. For example, there are significant differences in the nature and form of what is done with contemporary digital technologies and the pervasive manner in which they are coming to operate across most (if not all) spheres of life. There are also significant differences in scale and granularity. For example, the assemblages of digital tools, practices, processes and systems currently at large do not map seamlessly onto earlier analyses of the "mega machines" of the industrial age or the "mass consumption" of broadcast media. However prescient they might have been, Marx, Ellul and others were not contemplating AI or the Internet of Things in their arguments. Even the "internet" that Castells was writing about in the 1990s is a very different proposition to the online environments of today. Talk of the interconnected "open" potential of the "worldwide web" now seems an anachronism in our current era of proprietary platforms, tiered network access and closed apps. In short, digital sociology is addressing a very distinct technological landscape in contrast to the scholars of ten, fifty and 150 years ago.

Second, digital sociology allows us to redress specific blind spots in previous sociological work on technology. For instance, despite the example set by feminist writers, there is still plenty of scope to address issues of identity politics – not least how digital technology is entwined with issues of race, sexuality, disability and intersections therein. There is also a need to better address the computational basis of digital technology – not least the coded architectures of software, platforms and systems and the programmed nature of what digital technologies seem to "do" of their own accord. In addition, digital sociology is an opportunity to better address the intimate, personal and affective nature of contemporary technology use. With all facets of "the personal" being increasingly drawn into the digital devices and systems with which people interact, there is a need for scholarship that explores the issue of how we feel through technology and the intensity of experience as we encounter others online. Big ticket issues of society, economy and culture remain important, yet digital sociology can also be more introspective and intimate than previous sociological accounts of technology.

Third, digital sociology allows us to engage with digital technology on its own terms and in its own forms. As will be reiterated throughout this book, digital sociology is not simply the study of the digital as a topic; it also takes the digital to be an integral way of doing sociology. Digital sociology is practiced through digital resources. Sociologists can use an array of digital technologies to investigate, inquire, interact with and participate in their objects of study. They can now take advantage of an array of digital data and digital data analysis. Digital sociology is also performed through the media that it addresses, with sociological audiences and publics readily accessible through digital means. The notion of public sociology in the digital age has certainly moved on from acts of pamphleteering, giving public speeches and publishing journal articles.

Most excitingly, the current digital age could be seen as a time when ordinary people (and, by extension, sociologists) stand a realistic chance of "owning the means of production." Marx was not able to design, produce and distribute a socialist steam-powered mill. Yet it is not beyond the capacity of many sociologists to design and produce their own technologies, if only a simple website or app. Instead of striving only to imagine alternative technologies, it is now possible for sociologists to be involved in actually building and distributing them. Digital sociologists no longer have to speculate how things could be otherwise – they can make a tangible contribution to building (or more specifically coding) the future along different lines.

Conclusions

It is important to recognize that digital sociology is not a completely new or unprecedented development. Throughout its history, sociology has been a discipline that asks questions of the dominant technologies of the time. Yet digital sociology is clearly an important development in the sociology of the early twenty-first century. In short, it marks an opportunity for the discipline to look confidently beyond its roots in the industrial revolution and strive to make better sense of a post-industrial conditions that are now digitally distinct and often decidedly different. In this sense, the significance of digital sociology lies in its timing. This might not be a wholly new way of doing sociology, but it is a wholly necessary way of continuing to advance the discipline and maintain the relevance of sociological thought to contemporary society.

As such, digital sociology should be welcomed as a moment in the disciplinary development of sociology that sociologists of all dispositions can take full advantage of. This is perhaps the first time that sociological questions are being asked of the dominant technologies of the time by a generation of sociologists who are themselves immersed in the same technology. The theorists of the nineteenth and twentieth centuries had little first-hand experience of working with steam engines or nuclear reactors. In contrast, many of the leading digital sociologists are from a generation who were "born digital." As such, sociological work is increasingly assuming digital forms – these are times for blogging, tweeting and coding, as well as producing long-form monographs. In addition, it is significant that digital sociology comes at a time when sociological inquiry is being led by people who are not all white men. Given all these opportunities and openings, the next chapter will further explore the potential and promise of digital sociology. If we accept the basic premise of a digital sociology, then what might be the specific benefits of pursuing it? In short, "what can digital sociology do for us?"

2
Digital Sociology: Central Concerns, Concepts and Questions

Introduction

In many ways, the question of "What can digital sociology do for us?" is easily answered. In short, digital sociology allows us to make better sense of the digital world in which we live. To expand this a little, digital sociology provides a way of asking better questions of digital society – identifying problems, tensions and underlying issues that otherwise get glossed over amid the hyperbole that tends to cloud discussions of "new" technology. In doing this, digital sociology encourages a number of approaches that are worth further reflection. This chapter therefore explores three main areas of contention.

- First, digital sociology involves reframing the core technical features of contemporary technologies into sociological concerns. For example, as we shall go on to discuss, the idea of a "network" is usually seen in abstract, value-free terms – i.e. as the connecting of different nodes together. Yet, from a sociological point of view, the nature and significance of any network clearly alters when these nodes are people, institutions and machines.

- Second, digital sociology involves reusing and reconfiguring fundamental questions and concepts from the past 100 years of sociological thinking, as does any area of contemporary sociology. Digital sociologists are continuing an intellectual tradition that does not simply become irrelevant when confronted with a smartphone or an algorithm. Thus it is worth considering how digital researchers and writers are appropriating preceding sociological thinking and social theories and reassert them in powerful ways that address digital society.
- Third, digital sociology involves looking toward new forms of hybrid theory emerging from conflations of philosophy, computational sciences, design, politics, urban geography and other sources of critical thinking. While it rightly draws strength from its own disciplinary history, it also looks to get ideas from wherever it can. As we shall see, some of the most exciting and esoteric developments in digital critique originate a long way from traditional sources of sociological thinking.

So this is what digital sociology can do for us – pushing us outside of our comfort zones, prompting us to approach familiar aspects of the technological landscape in decidedly non-technical ways, and generally encouraging us to think in provocative, promiscuous and pragmatic ways. In this spirit, then, the first question that springs to mind is why we should cling on to the prefix of "digital" sociology? What is to be gained by distinguishing oneself as a *digital* sociologist?

Digital sociology as a "post-digital" take on "the digital"

As established in chapter 1, digital sociology approaches contemporary society as inherently digital and digitized. Of course, as we draw near to the 2020s, labeling something as "digital" or "non-digital" might come across as somewhat anachronistic – similar to how we now read 1990s talk of "cyberspace," "virtual communities" and "new media." We live in a world where digital technologies, systems and processes are barely noticeable and rarely seen as different. In many ways, "digital" now appears "a quintessentially twentieth – not twenty-first – century keyword" (Peters 2016: 93). Yet retaining the prefix of digital reflects a commitment to continuing to notice what has now largely become invisible. This is important if only because of the considerable disparities, differences and disjunctures that run throughout any digital society. Rather than being seamlessly woven into the fabric of everyday life, people's engagements with digital technologies vary dramatically around the world. As Sy Taffel (2016) points out, we are hardly living in a stable digital technoculture. As such, the label "digital sociology" reminds us that the digital is not simply now a case of "business as usual." This is not a topic that sociologists can afford to stop thinking critically about.

As such, one of the key ambitions of digital sociology is to make the digital visible, to highlight the flaws, glitches, gaps, seams and artifices. This chimes with the growing interest in "post-digital" perspectives – i.e. writing and research that looks beyond apparent technological progress and novelty and instead addresses a growing sense of "unease, fatigue, boredom and disillusionment" (Berry and Dieter 2015: 5) with contemporary technology-laden society. Thus, moving on from the initial rush of the digital, this requires scholarship where attention is focused on what is happening "after-the-digital" (Taffel 2016: 334).

Digital sociology, therefore, seeks to move beyond what Nathan Jurgenson (2012) calls the "digital dualism" of distinguishing between digital and analog, online and offline, real and virtual, and so on. Instead contemporary society is better understood as an entanglement of humanity, materiality and digitality. For example, it now makes increasing sense to describe urban environments as "code/spaces." Kitchin and Dodge (2011: 16) define this as where real-world spaces and software code "become mutually constituted, that is, produced through one another." Similarly, rather than being sometimes online and sometimes offline, most people are more accurately described as operating in a permanent state of "onlife" (Floridi 2014). As we shall discuss in chapter 3, a company such as Uber is simultaneously a technology platform, a transportation company *and* a labor organization. A "virtual community" is a blend of the physical and digital spaces, mediated sociability and in-personal social engagement (Maddox 2016). Digital sociology acknowledges and addresses the entangled nature of the material and the digital, people and machines.

Turning technical concepts into sociological concerns

Clearly, if Marx's writing about the handloom and steam engine is not directly transferable to making sense of Uber, then some new thinking is required. Against this background, one of the key thrusts of digital sociology is to (re)frame the technical characteristics of emerging digital technologies in sociological terms – i.e. cultural and social structures, social relationships and institutions, issues of power, conflict and control, political economy, and so on. In this respect, it is worth considering the ways in which digital sociologists have set about addressing the emerging technical concepts that underpin contemporary digital technologies, advancing the previous sociological theories of technology outlined in chapter 1 to highlight issues specific to contemporary digital technologies. Thus we can consider the following four key areas of writing in the recent digital sociology literature: (i) networks; (ii) platforms; (iii) data; and (iv) algorithms. Each of these examples illustrates the extension and recontextualization of previous sociological thinking for a digital age.

(i) Making sociological sense of "networks"

Networked computing – the connection of computers to permit the transfer of data – is a fundamental feature of digital technology. The idea of everything being connected to everything else in a flattened, non-hierarchical structure therefore drives commonsense understandings of digital technologies – for example, that the internet is inherently decentralized and democratic. As such, the notion of the social world being digitally networked has become "a way of life and a cultural norm" (Levina 2017: 127) that digital sociologists set out to problematize.

Of course, sociology has a long interest in the analysis of social networks, which was soon applied to emerging internet technologies during the 1990s. Most notable was Manuel Castells's (1996) description of the network society that he saw rising from the confluence of global capital and networked information technologies. Castells was particularly interested in the "networking logic" inherent in the reorganization of dominant societal functions and processes around networks rather than physical boundaries. He therefore developed a "network theory of power," describing how power in contemporary society is exercised through networks and how a reliance on dynamic networks was leading to the redefinition of time and space in everyday life.

Sociologists have subsequently extended and/or critiqued these ideas, all the time developing understandings of networked sociality. Alongside elaborations on network power are notions of network culture, network effects, network identity and network subjectivity. As Wendy Chun (2016) argues, the analytic appeal of networks lies in the promise to visualize otherwise incomprehensible complex flows of capital and power. In contrast to post-modernist celebrations of the unknownness of contemporary society, the idea of the network has become an increasingly popular "representational shorthand" (Jameson 1991: 36) for grasping otherwise unimaginable reconfigurations of society. Thus networks have quickly been established as a primary metaphor, method and theoretical tool of recent times.

Rather than taking networks at face value (for example, merely mapping online networks in terms of their size, shape and growth), digital sociology examines how networks "are being embedded into society and what conflicts this evokes" (Lovink 2011: 23). One key area of questioning is exploring how meanings are developed when the world is understood and arranged in terms of networks. For example, what are the social consequences of defining individuals on the basis of their interactions within networks? In what ways do networks "reassemble the social" (Chun 2015: 295) – for example, privileging the individual node while downplaying the role of community and wider society? What are the realities of network structures – where are inequalities, hierarchies, regulation and restrictions, and where are there disconnections, gaps, leaks and brokers (Cavanagh 2013)?

(ii) Making sociological sense of "platforms"

While today's technological infrastructure continues to compromise networks containing billions of devices, apps and software points, we are also seeing the increasing dominance of large "platforms" that are relatively centralized and closed. These platforms are often described as "intermediaries," bringing together customers, service providers, content producers and advertisers for social exchanges and economic interactions (Srnicek 2017). Such platforms infuse day-to-day digital practices and engagements. In much of the Western world, for example, dominant platforms include Google (search), Facebook (social networking) and Uber (taxi rides). Less obvious are cloud platforms renting out online storage space. All told, it is reckoned that most online traffic is concentrated on a dozen platforms and core servers owned by the likes of Microsoft, Google, Amazon and Apple (Scholz 2016).

Platforms constitute an arrangement of the digital ecosystem that differs substantially from the 1990s ideal of the open architecture worldwide web and therefore warrants close attention. Indeed, it is argued that we now live in a "platform society" where all areas of public and private life are permeated by platforms (van Dijck et al. 2018). One can certainly see a dominance of platforms in sectors of society such as news and journalism, retailing, hospitality and transportation. Van Dijck and his colleagues argue that these platforms have a profound impact on the way that social life is experienced and organized – from the changing neighborhood dynamics of Airbnb hotspots through to the (re)production and circulation of so-called fake news. In many ways, the largest platforms can be seen to "resemble states" in terms of their governance (Wark 2016).

The dominance of large-scale, monopolistic platforms is seen to derive from the "network effect" where "the more numerous the users who use a platform, the more valuable that platform becomes for everyone else" (Srnicek 2017: 45).

Thus users (and investors) are understandably attracted to the largest platforms. In turn, large numbers of users employ the data-driven business models of these platforms. Ostensibly "free" platforms such as Google and Facebook generate revenue by selling user data to advertisers. Similarly, "lean platforms" such as Uber and Airbnb are data-driven services that rent out assets that the company does not own. These economic characteristics are reflected in what has become termed "platform capitalism." Here, it is argued that these are not "tech" companies per se; rather, they are "businesses that increasingly rely on information technology, data, and the internet for their business models" (ibid.: 4). This means that a company such as Uber is a combination of a software platform, a business that seeks to extract and control data, a transportation company and a labor organization.

These latter characteristics raise a range of questions about the business practices of monopolistic platforms as well as the changing nature of work and labor that takes place around these platforms. Is a platform such as Uber promoting flexibility of work practices and increasing opportunities for previously underutilized/excluded elements of labor? Or is it reducing work stability and worker rights, as well as increasing discrimination through its reliance on data profiles, rating and reputation systems? As will be discussed in chapter 3, these questions are being addressed by growing numbers of digital sociologists around the world.

(iii) Making sociological sense of "data"

Running throughout these descriptions of networks and platforms is one of the key elements of contemporary digital society – "data." In a technical sense, digital data originates from a variety of different sources and takes a number of different forms. These include various forms of institutional monitoring and surveillance, data generated by routine operations of devices and software, and "user-generated" data volunteered by individuals while using digital technologies. The social significance of this lies in the computational "processing" work that predicts, models and distils data for human judgment. Once raw data begins to be processed it takes the form of more socially meaningful "data entities" – i.e. representations, models and calculations relating to "real-world things" such as people, places or products. In particular, the recent turn toward Big Data refers to these processes taking place on a mass, aggregated scale.

Recent work in digital sociology has therefore begun to challenge popular understandings of data as broadly neutral, objective and therefore non-problematic in nature. Instead, digital sociologists tend to approach data as political in nature – loaded with values, interests and assumptions that shape and limit what is done with it and by whom. As Gregg and Nafus (2017: 55) contend, "data play a major role in orchestrating contemporary power relations." In this sense, much of the sociological significance of digital data lies in its association with meaning-making – as Couldry and Hepp (2016: 213) put it, "what counts as social knowledge." This raises concerns over representation (with finite sets of characteristics being decided to "count" as a particular entity) alongside concerns over reductionism (with artificially neat boundaries and categories being drawn around data). As Halford et al. (2013: 180) conclude, "in short, the processes involved in naming, structuring and processing data ... are profoundly social with tremendous sociological implications."

Digital sociology also examines how digital data acts to define rather than simply describe social life. A key concept in this respect is the "social life" of digital data – i.e. the continual recirculation and reconstitution of data into different and new forms (Beer and Burrows 2013). This idea of a social life points to the fact that digital data is not used on a one-off basis. Instead, diverse sets of data are being continually combined and recombined, with different entities produced from varying iterations and calculations. As Andrew Webster (2013: 230) concludes, "data itself can take on its own life ... these data then travel, are transformed and are transcribed into novel 'derivative' forms."

(iv) Making sociological sense of "algorithms and automation"

The construction and use of algorithms has become a key way that digital data gets to shape everyday life. Whereas software engineers might see algorithms as a straightforward concept, from a social science perspective they are now a significant (albeit "invisible") concern (Mackenzie 2017). In a technical sense, an algorithm is simply a programmable series of logical steps that organize and act upon data to achieve specified outcomes, what is often described as a combination of "logic and control" (Kowalski 1979). First, a specific problem (and intended outcome) is formulated in computational terms (e.g. through the definition of variables, steps and indicators). This formulation is then "trained" on a body of existing data and its parameters adjusted and "tuned" to reach an accurate outcome more effectively. Eventually, the fully tuned algorithm will be incorporated into an application, giving it a capacity for automated reasoning and decision-making. This can be seen as an objective technical process, concerned with efficiency and elegance in reaching an outcome. Algorithms underpin most digital systems and practices that rely on decisions and predictions being made – from search engine results to credit scores, from driverless cars to economic forecasting. Algorithms, analytics and other forms of AI are all associated with the promise of bringing technical precision to what is an otherwise imprecise and unpredictable area of society, what Mattern (2016: 50) terms an allure of "instrumental rationality."

Of course, the sociological implications of algorithms are seen as far less straightforward, instead constituting "the insertion of procedure into human knowledge and social experience" (Gillespie 2016: 25). First, this has prompted much discussion among digital sociologists of the socially constructed nature of these processes, questioning how values are implicated in all stages of the algorithm design process. An obvious point to make from a sociological perspective, therefore, is that these processes of meaning-making are never wholly neutral, objective and "automated" but are fraught with problems and compromises, biases and omissions. There are clearly risks of reductionism in the disaggregation of complex social situations and contexts into neatly modeled and calculable problems that can be addressed through computational means (Mattern 2016). This is evident in the regular news media concerns over patterns of discrimination in algorithmic calculations and judgments – often resulting from biases in the assumptions of programmers and/or the data-sets that the algorithms are trained on. As such, many sociologists argue that discussion of "the algorithm" should not distract from the provider and designers. As Luciana Parisi (2013: 13) points out, the power that is now given up to algorithms throughout society belies their basis in "the indeterminacies of programming." For example, Google's much protected search algorithm is not an autonomous actor but actually the actions of Google (the company, its employees, its shareholders, and so on).

Second, digital sociologists are concerned with the implications and consequences of the insertion of algorithms throughout all areas of everyday life, leading to talk of algorithmic identity, algorithmic culture, algorithmic control and algorithmic governance. One key area of concern is how social actions and relations are conditioned by living in a world infused with algorithms. For example, as Frank Pasquale (2015) reasons, "we are increasingly pressured to adopt an algorithmic self, one conditioned to maximize exposure and approval." This leads to calls for increased transparency and "algorithmic accountability," thereby making algorithms more visible (and contestable) to the people on whom they impact.

Retaining and refining sociological questions and concerns

Running throughout these various discussions is a sense of holding up to sociological scrutiny "innovations" such as algorithms, data, platforms and networks. Digital sociology is not simply a matter of highlighting the social nature of these "new" things – rather, it is also concerned with unpacking the social issues and problems that are implicated in these digitizations. In this respect, digital sociology is driven by a number of familiar sociological questions and concerns. First, as reflected throughout chapter 1, is an interest in exploring the mutual shaping relationships between technology and society. This includes both what was referred to in chapter 1 as the social construction of technology and what Kennedy

(2017: 2) terms "the constitutive role of the digital." Wary of being branded technologically determinist, most sociologists remain keen to avoid any suggestion of the digital "impacting" directly on the social. Indeed, it can be rather comforting to suggest that digital society is largely a matter of "old wine in new bottles." Yet clearly the digital *does* impact on the social, albeit in inconsistent, unpredictable and compromised ways.

Making sense of "what is new here?" (as well as what remains the same) is something that digital sociologists therefore strive to "*make something of*, not shy away from" (Kennedy 2017, emphasis in original). This means that digital sociology pays close attention to the aspects of technology that people otherwise do not usually think about. In one sense, then, this involves a preoccupation with what might usually be considered the banal and mundane aspects of digital technology use. Distancing ourselves from everyday digital surroundings is notoriously difficult. Marshall McLuhan was fond of equating human awareness of media technologies to the way that a fish has no perception of the water in which it swims. In this sense, then, digital sociology follows C. Wright Mills's mantra to "make the familiar strange" and not to allow digital technology to recede into the background as something that is commonsense and unremarkable.

This said, digital sociologists also need to strive for the opposite effect – i.e. to make the strange familiar. Alongside the familiar devices and applications of our everyday lives, digital society involves highly complex systems and exotic digital practices. Here, digital sociologists have to come to terms quickly with unfamiliar new technologies and learn to engage with them as their expert users do. Bauman frames this as "familiarizing the unfamiliar" – i.e. "taming, domesticating, making manageable" (Bauman 2014: 98) what is otherwise well outside of our own experiences. Moving beyond the "shock of the new" is another important feature of digital sociology.

Of course, digital sociologists remain keen to address core disciplinary questions of social organization, social relations and social change. For example, digital sociology is intrinsically concerned with the politics and economics of digital society, not least the ways in which digital technologies play in complex, late modern social formations. Yet amid these macro-level concerns it is important to remain mindful that digital technology is encountered and experienced along deeply personal, intimate, human lines. A concurrent concern therefore remains with what Lina Dencik (2017) describes as "approach[ing] the digital in relation to practices and experiences." Indeed, digital sociology reminds us that digital technology is something that is experienced within distinct human contexts and with distinct human consequences. Digital technology use is entwined with people's feelings and emotions, their (dis)pleasures and (in)sensitivities. People are not merely extraneous variables in any instance of digital technology use. In particular, when foregrounding the human experience of digital technology use, digital sociology plays a key role in pushing back against the hyper-individualized discourses that pervade discussion of digital technology in most areas of life. As with all other areas of the discipline, digital sociology is inherently interested in looking beyond the individual.

In this sense, digital sociology is also concerned implicitly with the social structures that shape and constrain human experience of the digital. This has been a central feature of sociological thinking since Karl Marx's description of "men making their own history, but not making it as they please." Over 150 years later, Zygmunt Bauman framed such issues in terms of "sociological hermeneutics" – i.e. "the interpretation of human choices as manifestations of strategies constructed in response to the challenges of the socially shaped situation and where one has been placed in it" (Bauman 2014: 50–1). This moves digital sociology beyond simply documenting the human thoughts and actions that coalesce around digital technology and compels us also to consider questions of how these thoughts and actions came to be – as Bauman puts it, "the socially shaped conditions of people whose thoughts or actions we intend to understand/explain" (ibid.: 52).

As such, making full sense of individuals' responses to digital technologies requires a good understanding of social context, what Dencik (2017) terms situating digital technology "in contexts of social structures and interests." In this sense, the social contexts of people's engagements with digital technology are varied. If we take the mundane example of how digital technologies are used by university students, then an obvious set of contextual influences relates to the organizational structures of higher education – from timetables and the curriculum to wider imperatives such as increasing student numbers through to meeting the skills needs of industry. Other broader contexts relate to social class, race, ethnicity and gender; the subtle ways that neighborhoods bump up against campuses; the philosophies that different universities adopt (e.g. being "Ivy League" or "community-focused"). All of these issues can transcend individual "choices" in how digital technologies are engaged with and how they are used.

Finally, digital sociology does not strive to provide definitive answers to technological issues (indeed, there are few areas of sociology that could be said to pose questions that are definitively answerable). At best, sociological inquiry seeks to produce detailed, deep, thick and rich description that addresses the central question of "how has this world come about?" (Bauman 2014: 122). Digital sociology therefore tasks itself with pointing to the complexity of things rather than reaching oversimplified answers and solutions. The sociologist is keenly aware that there is no one definitive explanation, only different perspectives and truths. Thus, given this recognition of alternatives, an important supplementary question of any sociological inquiry is always "how might things be otherwise?" If we are not happy with the digital conditions that currently dominate, then what *do* we want?

The (re)use of social theory in digital sociology

Running alongside these questions and concerns is the use of social theory – in terms both of adapting (and extending) existing theory and/or being involved in new theory-building. In both respects, digital technology can be a tricky topic to theorize. On the one hand, it is proving remarkably adept at making use of "old" social theory, reappropriating ideas for digital contexts that would have been unimaginable at the time these ideas were originally formulated. This use of theory is pragmatic rather than dogmatic, with many digital sociologists following Manuel Castells's (2000) recommendation of "disposable theory" – i.e. recognizing theory as an essential tool but also acknowledging it as something to be discarded once it has outlived its usefulness in illuminating the substantive world. In these terms, any analysis of the digital is best arranged around an assemblage of theoretical perspectives as and when they best fit. This pragmatic use of theory is reflected by Amin and Thrift (2005: 222) when arguing that

> Theory has taken on a different style which has a lighter touch than of old. For a start, few now believe that one theory can cover the world (or save the world, for that matter). No particular theoretical approach, even in combination with others, can be used to gain a total grip on what's going on. Theory-making is a hybrid assemblage of testable propositions and probable explanations derived from sensings of the world, the world's persistent ways of talking back, and the effort of abstraction.

So it is important to remain mindful that there is no one correct theoretical stance to adopt when looking at digital society. Different theories are suited to different forms of questioning and specific areas of investigation. Take, for instance, the following two examples of theory use that have become popular in digital sociology of late.

(i) From Marx to digital Marxist theory

The case for recognizing Karl Marx as an early sociologist of technology is certainly bolstered by the (re)appropriation of Marxian theory throughout digital sociology. This can be seen in the growing popularity of twenty-first-century Marxian accounts of the digitally shaped nature of economic production, exploitation and class struggle under post-industrial capitalism. For example, Jodi Dean's (2005) notion of "communicative capitalism" has been taken up by digital sociologists to explore the commodified nature of communicative exchanges through digital media. Dean contends that the circulation of communication is now a prime means of generating value for data collectors, brokers, and analysts – therefore creating an imperative that things are continually being said online regardless of their substance. Similarly, as outlined previously, Nick Srnicek's (2017) critique of "platform capitalism" is proving a useful means of problematizing the growing dominance of monopolistic businesses that profit from the extraction and circulation of data as their raw material. This mode of capitalism involves firms generating network effects to consolidate power, sustained through enclosed ecosystems that bound users within closed apps and proprietary operating systems.

The adaptation of these ideas imbues digital sociology with some familiar Marxist concepts and concerns. Notably, traditional Marxist interests in political economy are evident in digital sociology critiques of the IT industry-related constellations of power now operating on a transnational scale (such as the rise of Silicon Valley and "Big Tech" as a global economic force). Framing mega-corporations such as Facebook in this manner has pushed many digital sociologists to set their work against new forms of capitalist relations that underpin the digital economy. "User-driven" platforms such as Facebook and YouTube are cast in a different light when approached as arrangements where capital owns the means of production *and* consumption. Thus it has proved useful for sociologists to consider how companies such as Facebook are developing strategies to control and profit from forms of digital (rather than material) production. For example, this leads to complex questions of what it means to be a social media "user" amid emerging online business models that seek to control and profit from the collective intelligence and attention of online groups (Koloğlugil 2015).

Elsewhere, digital sociologists are extending Marxist understandings of labor relations to make sense of virtual (rather than physical) forms of work. As will be discussed in chapter 3, this is prompting a rich vein of sociological writing on the rise of online "microwork" and the fragmented labor conditions of the so-called gig economy. This is also raising concerns over the ways in which digital technology users act increasingly like laborers, producing value through their individual content production, networked communication and cooperation with other users (Greaves 2015). In making sense of such issues, some digital sociologists have found particular value in applying autonomist Marxist theories of "immaterial labor" (Hardt and Negri 2001) to various virtual settings – examining the different forms of exploitation, immiseration, domination and struggle implicated in these ostensibly new forms of labor (see Koloğlugil 2015).

All these reworkings of Marxist theory therefore lend digital sociologists sharpened insights into some of the key conflicts and dialectic tensions inherent in digital society. For example, Marxian theory offers a convincing explanation for the apparently contradictory promise of platforms such as Google and Facebook to provide commons-based services rooted in human cooperation while at the same time profiting from online surveillance and ongoing exploitation of users (Fuchs and Dyer-Witheford 2013). Elsewhere, writing from a Marxist feminist perspective, Kylie Jarrett (2015) has highlighted how prevalent forms of immaterial digital labor have close parallels with other forms of domestic and consumer labour – unpaid and largely unseen forms of work that are unquestionably exploitative but also socially meaningful and individually enriching. For some commentators, such antagonisms point to a foreclosure of digital technology as a site of exploitation and social control (e.g. Dean 2005). Others, however, retain hope for possible resistance – pointing to counter-examples of proletarian struggle through digital networks and the prospect of "the communist/commonist internet" (Greaves 2015: 204). Either way, reworkings of Marxist theory continue to be a useful means for digital sociology to make sense of the power dynamics underpinning contemporary digital infrastructure.

(ii) From Foucault to post-Foucauldian theory

Besides these Marxian approaches, post-structuralist accounts of power and control are proving to be another popular appropriation of social theory in digital sociology. This often takes one of two forms. First are various reworkings of Michel Foucault's work on governmentality and disciplinary power to explore the surveillant characteristics of digital technologies. Indeed, comparisons continue to be made between contemporary digital technologies and Foucault's accounts of disciplinary power exercised through "panoptic" modes of control implicit in nineteenth-century social institutions such as schools and prisons. Foucault described the Panopticon as disaggregating the crowd into a collection of "separated individualities," with individuals' lives carefully monitored, collated and categorized. The awareness that any individual might be watched continuously therefore underpinned a state of self-regulation and the "automatic functioning" of power. While not constrained by "literal readings of Foucault's panoptic prison" (Elmer 2003: 232), critical scholars over the past thirty years have contended that the surveillant characteristics of networked digital technologies constitute a continuation of the disciplinary patterns implicit in the Panopticon (e.g. Poster 1990).

This use of Foucault's work continues to inform sociological accounts of varied panoptic arrangements ranging from school internet use (Hope 2016) to the activities of online advertisers and state agencies (Lyon 2014). Such work provides important reminders of "the use of pervasive personal data systems to systematically monitor people and groups in order to regulate, govern, monitor and influence their behavior" (Coté et al. 2016: 8). Conversely, Foucault's work has also been used to explore individuals' agentic uses of digital technologies. For example, wearables such as Google Glass and Fit-Bit have been conceptualized in terms of Foucault's "techniques of the self" – i.e. ways in which individuals look after themselves and improve their "thoughts, conduct, and ways of being" (Petitfils 2014: 39). Indeed, there is increasing sociological interest in the growing attraction of using personal devices for self-tracking and "participatory surveillance" (Lupton 2016; Graham and Sauter 2013).

Of course, digital sociologists have been quick to point to limitations in applying Foucauldian thinking to contemporary digital contexts. In particular, it is reasoned that Foucault's "architectural" forms of surveillance are superseded in the digital age by "infrastructural" forms of surveillance. These are decentralized forms of surveillance that are networked and involve remote forms of watching over data entities rather than physical bodies (Galič et al. 2017). A second wave of digital sociological work therefore turns to the work of Gilles Deleuze, especially ideas of rhizomatic networks and "control societies." While Deleuze did not live long enough to witness the rise of Google and Facebook, his ideas derive (at least implicitly) from the emergence of the 1980s and 1990s computerized bureaucratic society. Deleuze's writing certainly seem well suited to digital sociology. For example, his description of remote techniques of control superseding direct disciplinary techniques (Deleuze 1992) resonates with the rising significance of digital data throughout contemporary society. Deleuze described societies of control that were built around the monitoring of individuals' representations, what he termed the level of the "dividual." This is information that is deemed to represent an individual – what might be termed one's "data double" (Haggerty and Ericson 2000). These are not complete representations of an individual's physical self and their actions; instead they are composite representations and profiles of specific sets of technologically mediated behaviors (e.g. advertisers knowing someone only as a consumer with a history of online purchasing behaviors). Thus control in a Deleuzian society is exercised not by rendering people's "real" bodies docile but through attempts to monitor and control their data-bodies.

Approaching control and surveillance in these terms gives digital sociologists purchase on a range of prominent contemporary issues. Through Deleuze, for example, control can be seen as operating in an "ultrarapid" and "free-floating" manner across an assortment of networks that appear largely separate but ultimately connected (Galloway and Thacker 2007). Rather than being governed through a sense of being continually watched, individuals are subject to regular checks, permissions, the granting or denying of access, passwords and log-ins. Two important changes can be noted in comparison with the panoptic mode of control. First, it can be argued that the locus of power is relocated from immediate disciplinary institutions to remote databases, data profiles and data banks – what Latour (1987) termed "centers of calculation." Second, it can be argued that these forms of control become invisible and therefore imperceptible to most users.

These post-panoptic approaches have certainly pushed digital sociologists to address new assemblages of humans and technologies that now exercise forms of surveillance. Key areas of concern range from public awareness and critical understandings of how individuals are constantly disassembled and recomposed into data doubles (Lupton 2016) through to the inherent discrimination and inequalities inherent in data-based "sorting" (Leurs and Shepherd 2017). Poststructuralist theory therefore prompts digital sociologists to move away from descriptions of a ruthlessly efficient, all-seeing "Big Brother" toward the rather more incomplete and compromised realities of digital systems.

Moving beyond "pre-digital" theory

As these examples suggest, digital sociologists are making insightful and eclectic use of established social theory. Besides the work of Marx, Foucault and Deleuze, that of Erving Goffman on the presentation of self in everyday life continues to be popular with analysts of social media and identity, with 1950s concepts such as "frontstage," "backstage" and "facework" seen to translate neatly over to present-day LinkedIn profiles and Facebook feeds (Belk 2013). As Greenfield (2017: 14) puts it, "try to imagine ... the presentation of self without the selfie." Similarly, Pierre Bourdieu has found a renewed audience among scholars of digital inequalities. Here, the adaptation of concepts such as (online) "field" and (digital) "capital" has prompted talk of a "Bourdieusian digital sociology" (Ignatow and Robinson 2017: 956).

It is telling to consider why some "pre-digital" theorists have been picked up by digital scholars while other "big names" have not. It has been suggested that those theorists whose popularity endures all share a fluid, network-like sensibility in their ideas, underpinned by relative loose ontological assumptions (Sterne 2003). For example, Ignatow and Robinson (2017: 962) contend that "Bourdieu's ontological stance combining moderate realism and moderate social constructionism has proven a solid foundation for empirical [digital] sociology." Yet, notwithstanding the popularity of such authors, it is increasingly recognized that digital sociology should not be based wholly on the reappropriation of "pre-digital" theory. Indeed, it has been argued that relying on the application of "respective *a priori* theoretical commitments" leads only to limited understandings of digital technologies that are already socially ordered and organized by their producers and users (Brooker et al. 2017: 617). As Mackenzie Wark (2017 14) concludes, "perhaps it is no longer a time in which to use Foucault and Derrida to explain computing."

In another sense, then, digital sociology is proving to be a fertile site for the development of new theory – or at least a site where sociologists are exploring ways of making use of contemporary theories of digital society. Indeed, there is an array of recent theory that relates directly to the concerns and interests of digital sociology, albeit from writers who might not identify themselves as sociologists per se. This recent development of (post-)digital theoretical work has proven to be decidedly hybrid, collaborative and iterative in nature. Thus, rather than awaiting the emergence of a grand social theory for the digital age, digital sociologists are increasingly seeking out theoretical sustenance from across disciplinary boundaries. As Mackenzie Wark (2017 13) puts it, this is something that "general intellects might have to figure out together."

There are many writers and thinkers who fit this bill. For example, Wark highlights names such as Jodi Dean, Alexander Galloway and Wendy Chun as examples of such "general intellects" currently writing around the topics of digital media. Certainly, Galloway's work on interfaces, protocols and control deftly advances understandings of digital mediation and what the digital actually is. Similarly, Chun's historical expositions of the early internet have pushed understandings of online freedoms and constraints, as well the shifting nature of digital governance and organization. It is also well worth paying attention to the work of new media theorists such as Gert Lovink and Jussi Parikka in developing "network theories" and the notion of "media archaeology." Writers such as Ian Bogost and Lev Manovich have been working across areas such as computing, visual arts and design. Blending together philosophy, critical theory and media theory, Patricia Clough (2018) has also addressed extensively how digital technologies underpin an ever-altering sense of what it means to be human – especially in terms of the human body, subjectivity, affectivity and other "unconscious" processes. While these authors might not all be card-carrying sociologists, their work maps directly onto the concerns of digital sociology.

These theorists are notable for their broad terms of reference and knowledge bases, especially the ease with which they combine technical and philosophical concerns. Whereas social theory has always spanned disciplines such as philosophy, economics and sociology, the best digital theory-building of the past decade stems from social *and* computational origins. As such, it is increasingly apparent that digital sociologists need to develop a computational as well as a sociological imagination. This is not as daunting as it might sound. The computational and social sciences have a shared emphasis on analytical and logical thinking, as well as on developing deep theoretical understandings of complex systems. A field such as artificial intelligence draws as much on philosophy and linguistics as it does on mathematics and computer science. These are not areas of knowledge to which sociologists are wholly unsuited. Indeed, the most convincing current (post-)digital theorists are those who address digital philosophies and digital politics from the perspective of computational *and* human/social sciences. Writers such as Wark, Bogost and Lovink come from gamer, hacker and "hacktivist" backgrounds. Alexander Galloway is a philosopher with a long background in computer programing. Wendy Chun studied both systems design engineering and English literature – a mixture that she sees her work continuing to "combine and mutate" (Chun 2018). In short, the most insightful theoretical accounts of digital society seem to pay little regard to disciplinary boundaries.

The benefits of this approach are illustrated in Benjamin Bratton's (2016) recent account entitled *The Stack*. This ambitiously addresses the "planetary-scale computation" that has arisen over the past thirty years and the accompanying geopolitics that are now resulting. Bratton's thesis reflects his origins in sociology filtered through subsequent work in philosophy, design and computer sciences. This is theory-building that addresses the almost imperceptible machinations of global digital society. As such, it sets a high precedent for digital sociologists to follow. Tellingly Bratton's thesis is rooted in the computing metaphor of software "stacks," where layers of independent software components run on top of each other to form a complete platform. Approaching the digital world in these terms, Bratton outlines a complex multi-layered and modular "accidental megastructure" of computation, comprising six layers of the earth, cloud, city, address, interface and user.

There is much here that speaks directly to digital sociology. On a planetary level, for example, Bratton contrasts how the earth provides energetic and material sustenance for the technology of "The Stack" while also being increasingly diminished by the computational infrastructure that it sustains. In terms of the city layer, Bratton points to the reconstitution of urban spaces primarily to facilitate computationally driven consumption that is protected by computationally driven policing. In terms of users, Bratton reminds us of the growing dominance of non-human actors such as AI entities, bots, sensors, algorithms and animal users – all of which rely less on humans while humans rely increasingly on them. Yet, crucially, there is much in Bratton's thesis to challenge and unsettle digital sociologists, especially in terms of the computational elements of "The Stack." For example, he places great emphasis on the significance of software protocols and "deep" forms of mass digital address. Elsewhere, the significance of interfacial regimes reiterates the importance of interactions between humans and coded entities. These are all elements of the contemporary society on which it is less easy to gain sociological purchase.

These descriptions all convey a sense that governance and sovereignty are altering along lines that traditional sociological approaches are ill-equipped to accommodate. Bratton argues that, with the machine taking the place of familiar social structures such as the state, in short "we have no idea how to govern in this context" (2016: 213). This leads him to challenge the social sciences to jettison their "anthropocentric humanism" and "inadequate, immature" apprehensions over dehumanizing consequences of technology development and to suggest instead that the humanities and social sciences should focus attention on exploring opportunities to better integrate with the machine and design alternative components of this megastructure. As Bratton concludes, this requires directing efforts toward "not the Stack-we-have but the Stack-to-come."

Whether one agrees fully with this thesis or not, Bratton's provocations highlight the fact that sociology has a long way to go in making full sense of the digital. Of course, Bratton, Galloway, Chun et al. constitute an avant garde of digital theory-building which is already proving tremendously generative for digital sociologists to draw upon. Yet, while these new theoretical advances are clearly pertinent to the ongoing development of digital sociology, they also represent an implicit longer-term challenge to the relevance of a distinct digital sociology. These "computational philosophers" are amassing complex sets of ideas, all the time demonstrating that simply adding Foucault to Facebook is not a sufficient intellectual response to the complex machinations of the digital age. As such, there is a clear need for digital sociologists to strive to develop their *own* forms of powerful theorizing worthy of the computational twenty-first century.

Conclusions

At its heart, digital sociology marks a continuation of the sociological tradition. While the topics and subjects of inquiry might appear novel, digital sociologists are working in ways that are common to all areas of sociology. Digital sociology shares a commitment to asking difficult questions about issues such as structure and agency, power, domination, inequality and stratification. It is acutely aware of issues of political economy and cultural politics, and it is concerned with the privileging of individuals at the expense of the collective – the rise of private interests over public interests. These are concerns that persist across most aspects of sociology. As such, digital sociology can be seen as a space for sociologists of all different persuasions to come together.

Yet it important to see digital sociology as not merely a case of "more of the same." In many ways, it also marks a reconstitution of the sociological tradition. One of the core themes to emerge from this chapter is the need to combine sociological concerns with computational understandings. The lifeblood of digital sociology comes from a wide-ranging and fluid appropriation of ideas, theories and approaches.

This is an area of sociology that is eclectic, pragmatic and promiscuous in its reappropriation of theory (from all disciplines), while remaining rooted in the core sociological concerns that have developed since the 1900s. Digital sociologists should feel at ease in switching between continental *and* computational philosophy and in harboring interests in Marx *and* machine learning.

These past two chapters have concentrated on the precedents and foundations of digital sociology. It is now time to explore how these ideas are being put into practice. The next chapter therefore considers two important areas of empirical and theoretical scholarship of the digital by exploring recent sociological work in the areas of digital labor and digital race. What do all of the approaches discussed so far in this book look like when brought to bear on these two crucial areas of sociological inquiry – i.e. what it means to work and what it means to be black in contemporary society?

3
Digital Sociology in Action: Digital Labor and Digital Race

Introduction

Having explored the conceptual foundations of digital sociology, it is time to consider some practical examples of this scholarship of the digital. So what is the result of posing these questions, taking these theoretical approaches, and committing oneself to the critical scrutiny of digital technology? This chapter explores two illustrative examples of digital sociology inquiry – the areas of digital labor and digital race. Even for readers not usually drawn to the sociologies of work or race, these fast-growing areas of research and writing are useful ways to illustrate the practical application of concepts and approaches outlined in chapters 1 and 2.

Of course, there are many other topics of digital sociology inquiry that could be considered here. For example, there are strong bodies of research focusing on issues surrounding digital exclusion and the (non-)use of digital technologies among vulnerable and disadvantaged groups. There is growing interest in how engagements with digital technologies are stratified by social class, particularly those leading to unequal participation in domains such as health, education, social welfare and civic engagement. There is also a rich empirical literature around issues of gender and sexuality in the digital age, from moral panics over teenage "sexting" to online communities of relatively benign Furries and clearly less benign Incels. And there is an increasing number of empirical accounts of the digitization of various institutions across society, from families to schools, and from justice systems to religion. These include nuanced sociological investigations of the changing nature of digital parenting, the division of digital domestic labor, and the altered nature of online knowledge and authority.

All of these areas – and others – are worth exploring in order to get a full sense of digital sociology scholarship. For the time being, however, this chapter will focus specifically on how digital sociologists are making sense of two topics that are of long-standing sociological interest – (i) work and employment and (ii) race and ethnicity. Recent studies in each of these areas of inquiry show how researchers and writers are extending preceding "pre-digital" sociological literatures in these areas. In particular, the chapter will reflect on what these studies can tell us about the distinctly digital nature of these issues. In short, what is digital sociology adding to existing understandings of societal issues that are already widely discussed and known about?

Sociological studies of digital labor

We can first turn our attention to matters of work and employment. A popular expectation during the last few decades of the twentieth century was that new technologies would lessen the need for hard work and generally improve people's working lives. Indeed, technology marketing continues to promote a sense that new and exciting things simply get "done" through digital technologies without the need for work at all. As such, many people tend not to think about digital technology use specifically in terms of work and labor. Yet the ongoing digitization of contemporary society clearly involves substantial amounts of mental and manual labor alongside significant shifts in the coordination and distribution of work.

Despite this lack of popular consideration, the fast-changing nature of work in the digital age has emerged as a prominent interest within digital sociology, often in the guise of studies of "digital labor." This is research and writing that questions how digital technologies are altering work patterns in established jobs and professions, as well as how digital technologies underpin ostensibly new forms of distributed work. There is also considerable interest in the ways in which value is created from the unpaid actions of mass online audiences. Thus digital sociologists are keenly exploring questions of "what it means to 'labor' in the digital economy" (Kuehn and Corrigan 2013). Who is engaging in digital forms of work, under what conditions and with what outcomes? To what extent are workers being advantaged or exploited, empowered or alienated? How is such work experienced, and what inequalities are evident?

(i) The digitization of traditional work

First is the question of how digital technologies are altering traditional jobs and professions. Here, researchers have documented ways in which various existing jobs and professions are being reshaped by digital processes and practices. Take, for instance, what Nicole Cohen (2015a: 100) terms the "reformatting of journalism in a digital age" – i.e. how journalists' work is increasingly fragmented, automated and sped up by digital technologies. Cohen and others highlight a wide range of changes to consider. For example, news production has now reached a stage where reporting can be automated, with some sport, financial and weather bulletins now fully computer-generated. Other reporting is drawn from so-called content farms employing low-paid freelancers to quickly rewrite text drawn from data-mining and content aggregation. News outlets are also eager to rely on online audiences as a source of unpaid content – making increasing use of "citizen journalism" and invited bloggers as well as audience comments and feedback.

These developments all have considerable bearing on the nature of contemporary journalism. In particular, Cohen argues that journalistic output is now subject to continuous analytic scrutiny. This ranges from automated assessments of "newsworthiness" to real-time analysis of the audience "traffic" and "engagement." Cohen describes how journalists' writing decisions are disciplined by these meta data and analytics, and how they feel compelled to produce stories that reflect well in terms of "clicks" and "stickiness." As Cohen (2015a: 113) concludes, "digital production processes are undermining journalism as a creative endeavor, challenging independence and autonomy."

Similar issues and tensions are apparent across many other forms of professional work. For example, Selwyn et al. (2017) point to pervasive ways in which digital technologies are reshaping the work of schoolteachers. This includes the standardization of teaching activities and actions through the use of online "teacher-proof" pre-scripted lesson plans. Teachers are also increasingly working alongside content "recommender systems" and automated grading systems. Echoing the use of newsroom metrics, digital technologies further underpin a steady quantification and measurement of teachers' work – not least the growing use of "learning analytics" and other monitoring and feedback tools. Finally, Selwyn (2016: 21) notes that "perhaps the most significant trend is the digital expansion of schoolwork across space and time," with teachers increasingly expected to interact with students, parents and colleagues outside what were once considered "school hours."

Such uses of digital technology could be seen as bringing modern efficiencies to otherwise traditional work settings of the newsroom and classroom. Other research suggests that newsroom analytics can act as a source of motivation and reassurance for some journalists, with the nature of compliance varying considerably between different work contexts (Bunce 2018; Petre 2015). Yet digital sociology reminds us that there is also much to be wary of. For example, the developments detailed by Cohen and Selwyn mostly involve the fragmentation of professional work, leaving the conception of what should be complex and creative tasks increasingly separated from their execution. Enthusiasms for the capacity of digital technologies to "unbundle" work processes tend to gloss over the likelihood of deskilling highly trained professionals through persistent standardization and separation of work and the subversion of judgment and expertise. Cohen's and Selwyn's analyses quickly reach the conclusion that these are not technological changes that advantage the majority of journalists and teachers. Indeed, once tacit knowledge is devalued and tasks are standardized, they can be readily separated from specialized workers and then outsourced and/or automated. These studies provide useful counterpoints to the hype of the twenty-first-century workplace. Indeed, many technological changes in contemporary workplaces could be said to be hastening the reconstitution of labor processes, from ones directed by workers to ones controlled by managers, administrators and commercial outside interests. Digital sociology therefore raises the suggestion that what appear to be technical efficiencies might actually act to increase alienation and disengagement of workers from their tasks. While not a root cause of these problems, digital technologies nevertheless amplify pressures of performativity, auditing, deskilling, life–work balance and the casualization of labor. As such, these are trends that digital sociology is proving well able to problematize.

(ii) New forms of distributed, discrete work

Alongside the digitization of "traditional" work, digital labor scholars are exploring new forms of distributed, automated and fragmented work – in particular the crowdsourcing of information-based "microwork" and digitally coordinated freelancing in the "gig economy." These "irregular forms of labor" (Sevignani 2013: 130) all reflect a growing trend for the distribution of work and the coordination of workers on a mass scale through networked technologies.

For example, the distribution and coordination of "microwork" involves small segments of much larger projects being contracted separately at low cost to dispersed individuals around the world (Walker 2012). Prominent microwork platforms with names such as Clickworker and Cloudfactory boast thousands of registered workers. The best known (and most widely researched) of these is Amazon's "Mechanical Turk" (AMT) platform. Established in 2005, AMT is marketed as offering "access [to] a global, on-demand, 24 × 7 workforce" estimated at over one million so-called Turkers whom any "Requester" can pre-test and then contract to carry out the task. Significantly, this model of online outsourcing derived initially from the IT industry's need to process large amounts of unstructured data. Indeed, microworkers continue to provide the bulk of "infrastructure labor" that sustains the running of the internet. These include low-paid evaluators who manually filter and moderate content, pre-test algorithms and test code. Demand for cheap online data work has since expanded to many other information- and data-related domains, taking in academic researchers looking for cheap/plentiful sources of experimental subjects.

Another form of digital labor is the freelance gig economy, most familiar in the guise of popular ride-sharing services (Uber, Lyft), delivery services (Deliveroo, Foodora), and services providing household work and chores (TaskRabbit). These platforms are touted as supporting the thriving "on-demand economy," recasting workers as "micro-entrepreneurs" who "are their own bosses, work flexible hours, and control nearly everything about the platform experience" (Schor and Attwood-Charles 2017). While the eventual tasks are usually physical in nature (e.g. driving cars, cycle couriering, cleaning houses), all exchanges take place through proprietary apps that link workers to specific tasks and assignments. As Malin and Chandler (2017: 382) describe the platform-based nature of Uber: "relying on mobile telephones' locative and messaging capacities, the entire exchange, including communications, payment, and post-drive ratings of both driver and passenger, takes place through these digital apps."

Looking beyond industry and investor enthusiasms for platforms such as Uber and AMT, an obvious sociological question is the extent to which these new forms of labor constitute the empowerment or the exploitation of workers. On the face of it, these are underpaid forms of employment with minimal worker protections and rights. Yet digital labor scholars are finding that, while microwork and gig work might appear low-skilled and exploitative, these are more complex forms of labor than might appear. For example, Irani (2017) reports that more than half of the "most active" Amazon Turkers have college degrees. As well as earning income, some workers value being able to make strategic use of platforms to supplement "downtime" in their primary careers and professions. Neither is this wholly unpleasurable work: studies suggest that microworkers experience intense "flow-like" experiences of absorption and enjoyment "lead[ing] to complete immersion in the tasks" (Bucher and Fieseler 2017: 1870) akin to playing computer games.

Empirical studies also give a sense of workers' tactical engagement with these labor conditions. Neha Gupta reports Indian Turkers setting up online forums to informally induct new members, set ethical norms, provide advice and social support, alert others to good jobs, review requesters and air grievances (Gupta et al. 2014). Similarly, Rosenblat and Stark (2016: 3759) found Uber drivers developing forums "to learn tricks and tips for success on Uber's platform; compare and share practices and screenshots; complain socially about passengers and the company; and debate Uber's practices, including discrepancies between the passenger and driver apps." Yet these instances of social capital building and sousveillance are limited. As Irani (2017: 3) concludes, "the dispersion of workers across geographies, however, may dampen workers' ability to identify with one another and take collective action."

Another recurring sociological concern is the technology-based control of these workers – i.e. "their increased subordination and dependence on the platforms to which they are tied" (Casilli 2017: 2068). For example, studies have explored how promises of increased freedom and flexibility for Uber and Lyft drivers are contradicted by "softer" and less visible forms of automated surveillance and algorithmic analysis (Shapiro 2018). Of particular significance are data-based forms of control, with platforms using information asymmetries to influence workers' decision-making. For example, Shapiro's research highlights how "remote company dispatchers maintain omniscient views of worker fleets on real-time digital maps," while providing drivers partial access to information as a means of "nudging" them toward accepting particular tasks that fulfil the platform's needs.

Another prominent finding is the differentiation of these workers along lines of class, race and geography. Such disparities are evident in a number of different forms. For example, studies of TaskRabbit use in Chicago found that "providers" were less likely to accept offers of work from consumers with addresses in low socioeconomic areas of the city. Moreover, the providers who did work in these areas tended to demand higher rates for their services (Thebault-Spieker et al. 2015). Elsewhere, Malin and Chandler (2017) suggest the increased likelihood of rides being cancelled on Uber after passengers see profiles of drivers of color. Similarly, the distribution of microwork opportunities is found to be tempered by what Mark Graham terms "the liability of foreignness" (Graham et al. 2017: 158). Analysis of microwork platforms set up in Hispanic, African and Asian regions notes consistent customer favoring of workers perceived as well-educated, first-language speakers. This contrasts with the negative stereotyping of workers from South Asia and Africa in terms of ethicized assumptions of work ethic and language skills (Graham et al. 2017; Galperin and Greppi 2017). As Irani (2013) concludes, these are "differences that build on old and gendered divisions of labor that, through infrastructure, can be reproduced at global scales."

(iii) Social media as sites of "free labor"

A third strand of digital labor literature relates to the ways in which value is created from the unpaid actions of online audiences. This is what Terranova (2000) describes as "free labor" – i.e. forms of online engagement "in which exploitation, pleasure, work and leisure become harder to distinguish" (Aroles 2014: 145). One prominent issue for digital labor scholars consists of the ways in which individuals' use of social media creates value that can be appropriated by other parties for profit generation (Bodle 2016). For example, the business model of Facebook relies on mining and selling data to third parties, both for targeted advertising on the platform and for detailed consumer profiling. In addition, content contributed to Facebook functions to create opinions, tastes, subjectivities and other cultural content that can be commercially profited from (Coté and Pybus 2011). As Fuchs and Sevignani (2013: 267) conclude, "Facebook labor creates commodities and profits. It is therefore productive work. It is however unpaid work."

Another form of free labor is the "co-creative labor" that users undertake in the course of their internet use (Banks and Deuze 2009). One example of this is the extensive amateur creation of online content by fans of popular cultural products such as films, comic books and sports teams. Online genres of fan fiction, fan art and fan "modding" have been noted as unofficial forms of publicity and marketing for the culture industries – adding "value to mass-produced commodities" in ways that are "worthy of compensation" (De Kosnik 2013: 110). Indeed, many firms now strive deliberately to have their brands and products featured in content being created and shared by social media users. Of course, for many users, social media activities might not seem like work. Indeed, this free labor is often celebrated as a voluntary, altruistic and empowering form of self-expression and creativity (see Lindgren 2017; Shullenberger 2014). Yet social media rely on users spending considerable amounts of time and effort to consume *and* produce content. Whether they see themselves as working or not, most social media users are therefore engaged in cognitive, communicative and cooperative activities that lead to the creation of new "immaterial" products.

Another type of free labor relates to activities that users pursue in the expectation of their subsequently leading to paid work. This has been described as "hope labor" – i.e. "un- or under-compensated work carried out in the present, often for experience or exposure, in the hope that future employment opportunities may follow" (Kuehn and Corrigan 2013). Examples here include individuals writing regular product reviews for sites such as Amazon or sports blogs for syndicated websites, submitting speculative designs to sites such as Threadless, and self-producing shows for video-sharing sites such as YouTube. All of these activities involve unpaid work undertaken "as a future-oriented investment" (ibid.) in the hope of being talent-spotted. These forms of "hope labor" mark a reframing of unpaid work as an expected (if not desirable) element of the digital economy.

Such aspirational activities are driven by the success of small numbers of social media users who have been able to monetize their content successfully. For example, many free-laborers aspire to the status of so-called influencers or micro-celebrities (Abidin 2017). These are individuals producing regular online content related particularly to their own personal lifestyles as well as particular topics such as fashion, beauty tips and gaming. Research into these forms of labor highlight the considerable demands of such work – not least the "contrived authenticity" and "calibrated amateurism" of maintaining an appearance of not being a paid professional (ibid.). For example, Duffy and Wissinger (2017) highlight stressful forms of "emotional labor, self-branding labor, and an always-on mode of entrepreneurial labor" implicit in in these forms of social media work. Elsewhere, Duffy (2017) notes recurring inequalities of gender, class and status evident in terms of which YouTubers and Instagrammers succeed in developing profitable careers. As with the microwork and gig work described earlier, while all internet users might have access to the same platforms, these forms of digital labor are certainly not equitable or democratic.

Digital labor – recurring themes and issues

One of the key themes in digital labor scholarship is a question that has recurred throughout our discussions – i.e. "what is new here?" To what extent does microwork, the gig economy, influencers and automated copy-editing represent "a reimagined capitalism" (Schor and Attwood-Charles 2017)? Conversely, in what ways are these merely continuations of long-standing economic and societal conditions? Digital labor scholars are quick to acknowledge that many of the tensions and dynamics associated with these forms of digital labor have existed for some time. For example, practices of freelancing, piecework, unpaid apprenticeships and creative workers not making money from their art are well established (Cohen 2015b). As the sociological literatures on prosumption (Ritzer 1993) and coproduction (Dujarier 2015) remind us, some of the most successful companies over the past fifty years (McDonald's, Ikea) have relied on putting consumers to work. There are clear similarities between unpaid domestic work and the ways in which digital capitalism is reliant on the capture and use of seemingly voluntary and unpaid activities undertaken by digital media users (Jarrett 2015). Thus while these instances of digital labor might involve altered configurations of the means of production, many of the unequal relations of production appear to remain intact (Schor and Attwood-Charles 2017).

Clearly, then, the rise of digital labor is entwined with wider general "reorganizations of work" implicit in post-industrial transitions (Flecker et al. 2017). The development of Facebook, Uber and AMT continue decades-old trends such as declining direct employment, the rise of "precarious" employment and casualized labor, and the diminishment of workers' rights. Similarly, the ways in which digital technologies are used in traditional workplaces such as newsrooms and schools reflect broader entrenchments across all employment sectors of strategies of efficiency, standardization, "new managerialism" and "corporate reform." In all these ways, then, our understandings of digital labor need to be contextualized in terms of these preceding economic and social logics.

In this sense, digital sociology is proving a useful means of moving debates over digital labor beyond simplistic questions of whether these forms of work are "good" or "bad." Any criticism is tempered by the fact that microworking, the gig economy, unpaid content creation and social media influencing appear to be practices in which some individuals engage by choice. Whether in terms of journalists' motivational use of metrics or social media users' creation of content, it could be argued that "control ultimately hinges on workers' willingness to conform to the calculative rationalities that companies project onto them" (Shapiro 2018). Rather than wholly dismissing this work as forms of servitude and exploitation, digital labor scholars are keen to reflect on why these practices are increasing in prominence. Thus much of the writing and research outlined above strives to deepen understandings of "the value that users might extract from their own labor" (Hughes 2014: 650). In this sense, these forms of work are clearly of personal benefit for many individuals that cannot be dismissed out of hand. There is a doubled-edged, contradictory nature to such work. It is socially meaningful but also economically vital, individually enriching but also individually exploitative (Jarrett 2015).

Yet, notwithstanding the need for a balanced perspective, digital sociology does raise a number of wider concerns over digital labor. First are the ways in which many of these digital settings obscure the labor that is being carried out – as Trebor Scholz (2013: 2) puts it, these are activities that do not "feel, look, or smell like labor at all." Social media, smartphones and other personal technologies are certainly effective means of lulling individuals into not feeling as if they are working, even when they plainly are. These are forms of technology use that are framed as a form of play rather than work (Scholz 2013) – for example, something that is "cool," "fun" and led by individual "passions" (Jarrett 2015).

These are also technologies that reframe labor in highly individualized, solitary and solipsistic terms. Many of the forms of digital labor just described place responsibility and risk firmly on individual workers rather than on employers (many of whom refuse to recognize themselves as employers at all). This leads to situations where individuals are alienated not only from productive processes and the products being created but also from other workers. Thus any sense of work being undertaken in collective or collegial ways is obscured, leading to a curtailed sense of workers' collective rights and protections as well as a diminished dignity of labor (Fish and Srinivasan 2012). In this sense, digital labor scholarship brings us back to many of the central concerns of digital sociology highlighted in chapters 1 and 2 – i.e. interplays between structure and agency, social relations and social change, and the importance of seeing digital technology in terms of human experiences.

Sociological studies of digital race

The digital labor literature certainly provides a critical rejoinder to the digital optimism of the 1990s and 2000s. In particular, these new forms of digital labor contradict the idea of digital technologies leading to fairer, more democratic and more just social processes. As Nakamura and Chow-White (2013: 7) put it, one of the enduring promises of the digital age has been "technology with a radical form of agency, endowed with the capacity ... to create an ideal 'information society' where everyone is radically equal." Yet, as the realities of working in digital "gigs" and "tasks" illustrate, this is clearly not turning out to be the case. The digital labor studies just reviewed point to a number of inequalities, not least issues of race. In times when African-American Uber drivers and Amazon Turkers from South Asia are negatively prejudged and profiled by their prospective customers, race clearly remains an issue that is interwoven throughout digital labor. Indeed, the topic of race offers a second important illustration of the breadth and depth of digital sociology.

Tellingly, academic discussions of digital technologies over much of the past thirty years have been notably non-racialized in nature. This stems partly from their coincidence with what has been termed the "post-racial" turn. This is the "commonplace yet hubristic ideological contention that contemporary liberal democracies have transcended the logics of race and racism" (Valluvan 2016: 2242). Thus social researchers became interested in digital technologies and the internet around the same time that many North American and European commentators were considering the possibilities of their countries moving "beyond race" and evolving into multicultural societies with "color-blind" institutions.

Until recently, the eagerness of academics to approach new digital technologies in a color-blind manner attracted little reflection or concern. After all, many researchers involved in social studies of digital media would consider themselves to be liberally inclined scholars hopeful about a racism-free future. It has been all too easy to presume that there is no racism to be found. However, this stance is now being challenged by sociologists attuned to the sharply racialized nature of contemporary digital life. These scholars are contributing to a critical literature on what might be termed "digital race" – i.e. considerations of how race is implicit in people's encounters and experiences of digital technology across various facets of everyday life. This is a particularly strident area of digital sociology, unafraid to call out the "color-blind racism" of other digital researchers willfully blind to racial dimensions of their chosen topics of study (Daniels 2015).

As such, digital race is proving a compelling example of digital sociology making a distinct and vital contribution to contemporary sociology.

(i) Moving beyond the "digital divide"

As just implied, the recent critical literature on digital race certainly marks a reaction to the weaknesses of preceding scholarship. In particular, digital race researchers are keen to distance themselves from the treatment of race developed in social research purporting to address the topics of digital inequalities and digital divides. Over the past thirty years digital divide studies have regularly pointed to race – alongside age, gender and social class – as a significant factor in the ongoing inequalities of opportunity and outcome associated with digital technology access and use. The digital divide literature since the 1990s has highlighted how people's engagements with digital technologies such as computers and the internet have remained patterned by race over time, even in high-tech regions of North America and Europe. In the US, for example, the authoritative Pew "Internet & American Life" program reports that "home broadband use" remains differentiated in favor of whites (78 percent of adults) as compared to black (65 percent) and Hispanic (58 percent) adults. So, while headline figures might appear to be improving, the race-related digital divide is acknowledged as far from being "bridged."

Such evidence continues to be used widely in policy and academic circles. Yet for many digital sociologists this research provides a dangerously restricted view of race and technology. A strong case can be made that people's encounters with digital media cannot be reduced simply to categories of being "users" or "non-users," digital "haves" or "have nots." For example, people's experiences of digital engagement and participation vary dramatically and do not result in consistent levels of power sharing or empowerment (Andrejevic 2007). Their interactions with what might appear to be the same digital technology will depend considerably on their circumstances, context and racialized agency. As Tressie McMillan Cottom (2016: 214) reasons, the idea of being on the right or wrong side of a "digital divide" does "not go far enough to capture the various intersections of privilege, access, and power that operate online and offline simultaneously and which can also be mutually constitutive."

Against this background, the argument is now being made that digital divide research is limited by its focus on correlations and individual attributions rather than on the more complex structural stratifications of people's digital choices and actions. Portraying groups of African Americans as stranded on the "wrong side" of a divide "leaves the way race is embedded in structures, industry, and the very idea of the internet largely unexamined" (Daniels 2015: 1377). In contrast to depicting race-related divides and digital inequalities, then, many digital sociologists position themselves as starting from the point that race is not a hard-and-fast variable but is socially constructed. As such, this is scholarship focused explicitly on the inherently racialized dimensions of digital culture, economics and politics and challenges the ways in which "whiteness" is continually affirmed as normative across the important features of digital society (Nakayama 2017). From these starting points, then, digital race research sets out to portray the dynamics of contemporary digital society in more nuanced and complex ways than has previously been the case.

(ii) Race and online interactions

The literature on digital race examines the racialized nature of digital media along a number of different lines. This includes work addressing the dynamics of online interactions. Early research in this area tended to focus on the visual (mis)representation of race in websites, videogames and user interfaces. However, this has shifted throughout the 2010s to addressing the actions and consequences of people's online interactions. As Nakamura and Chow-White (2013) reason, digital media are no longer texts that are consumed passively. Instead, their main social function is processual rather than visual, thereby demanding scrutiny of the racialized nature of what is being done to people through digital media, rather than what digital media show and represent.

These concerns have prompted various studies of how discrimination is enacted through digital media. For example, a series of studies from Harvard researchers detailed the systematic discrimination of African Americans on the Airbnb room-sharing platform. This found, for example, properties listed with pictures of black landlords receiving nightly rates that were 12 percent lower than those for proprietors depicted as not black (Edelman and Luca 2014). Similarly, guests with typically African-American names were 16 percent more likely to be rejected by hosts (Edelman et al. 2016). Other research reports that Airbnb hosts in areas with predominantly white populations receive better ratings and demand higher prices (Cansoy and Schor 2016). Crucially, the commodified market-like nature of exchanges means that such platforms do little to counter such differentiation. Indeed, as Niesen (2016: 173) concluded with regard to specified racial preferences on dating and hook-up sites such as Tinder, eHarmony and Grindr, "bigotry is generated through the labor of users themselves."

Alongside these forms of transactional discrimination, digital race research highlights various ways that digital media support direct harassment of people of color. This is explored in studies of online racialized harassment and hate speech, ranging from "cloaked" websites (Daniels 2009) to Twitter (Hardaker and McGlashan 2016). This research lends weight to Nakayama's (2017) contention that online communication tends to amplify harassment and vilification through a combination of anonymity, interactivity and access to a global audience. These shifts in social distance and scale mean that online environments can quickly become perceived by users as places where "expressing socially unacceptable views" can be "more socially acceptable" (Stein 2016: 29). Other studies find these traits evident in online gaming communities. For example, Kishonna Gray's (2016: 355) research on Twitch gaming communities describes in detail how gamers of color encounter sustained "racism and harassment by other gamers" alongside the regular performances of "hegemonic Whiteness and masculinity." Gray's work illustrates how these practices are quickly normalized, accepted as legitimate, and embedded in the continued cultural practices within online gaming.

One important theme throughout these studies is how such discriminations do not arise solely from the actions of individual users. Instead this research highlights ways in which applications and platforms are configured in ways that prompt and perpetuate racialized dynamics. For example, Matamoros-Fernández's (2017) description of "platformed racism" details how popular platforms such as Facebook are configured and implemented in ways that perpetuate whiteness. This ranges from their internal policies and external terms of service (which usually adhere to white and/or Western values and ethics) through to the commercially driven reuse of platform data. This latter point was illustrated by Facebook's development of an "ethnic affinity" indicator based on users' prior tracked engagement with specific pages and content. This data was sold to advertisers wanting to target their products only to particular ethnic groups. As Matamoros-Fernández (ibid.: 933) concluded, while Facebook acted on what was computationally possible, "the business orientation of this technical functionality overlooked its potentiality to be discriminatory."

Indeed, the racialized nature of computational processes and algorithmically determined encounters is a growing area of academic interest. Critical scholars have long noted racial differences in terms of "algorithmic visibility" (Introna and Nissenbaum 2000) and what Gandy (1993) terms the "panoptic sort" of online data. Here it is argued that data-based practices designed to classify, sort and evaluate populations inevitably reproduce existing racial inequalities, while then going on to generate new modes of racial discrimination through the cumulative recirculation and recombination of already racialized categories – what Gandy terms a "matrix of multiplication." In this vein, current scholars have begun to detail algorithmic racial exclusion on online dating sites (Robnett and Felliciano 2011), the biases inherent in biometrics and facial recognition software (Browne 2010), and the racist misrecognitions that are naturalized into the coding processes informing Google's search engine algorithms (Noble 2018). All these studies confirm the argument, as Gillborn et al. (2018: 158) observe, that computer-generated models and calculations are compromised by "hidden assumptions that frequently encode racist perspectives beneath the façade of supposed quantitative objectivity."

Some studies also examine the human basis of what might appear to be machine-led automated discrimination. For example, as was described earlier, much of the content moderation and filtering on platforms such as Facebook is carried out by microworkers rather than by automated systems. While platforms purport not to permit racist content, any actions to block or censor often depend on "complicated matters of judgment" on the part of these workers (Roberts 2016: 148). Studies of those involved in "commercial content moderation" point to the often racialized outcomes of these processes, as low-paid workers (often in located in low-income countries) are tasked with making rapid interpretations of their employers' internal policies and commercial imperatives. These are commercial environments where distasteful, sensationalist and disturbing content can be popular and profitable – as Roberts (ibid.: 151) notes bluntly, "racist content sells." As a result, these workers find themselves continually balancing their censorious role with their personal values and the underlying pressure of the profit motives of their employers.

(iii) Race and the digital formation of collective identity

Another strand of research examines the changing nature of collective identity formation and resistance through people's use of social media platforms. Whereas early internet research often focused on individuals' self-presentation and identity performance, these recent studies have shifted attention toward collective actions and the formation of social media publics. One much researched case considered the complex ways in which social media was used in the aftermath of the 2014 police killing of Michael Brown in the US town of Ferguson. As is now common in such events, digital media proved a significant conduit for the public exchange of information and commentary. Subsequent studies have therefore explored the roles that platforms such as Facebook, YouTube, Instagram, Tumblr, Vine and Twitter played in supporting collective reflection and commemorative "memory work" (Smit et al. 2017). In particular, this highlights how the operational logics and practices of platforms work to popularize particular narratives and representations over others. For example, Smit and his colleagues detail how collective memories of the Ferguson shooting were shaped by platform logics of privileging "sharable" iconic images, brief emotive slogans, simplified ideas and polarized arguments. As these researchers conclude, social media enabled the widespread co-construction of simplified discourses in lieu of "the complexities of the issues at hand" (ibid.: 19).

Another focus of this research is the collective use of hashtags to support awareness raising and protest – what has been termed "hash-tag publics" (Rambukkana 2015). This is most prevalent in the form of racially related hash-tags or "black tags" (Sharma 2013) such as #IfTheyGunnedMeDown, #HandsUpDontShoot and #BlackLivesMatter. The widespread use of such hash-tags has been explored in a number of studies. For example, Harlow and Benbrook's (2018) examination of the use of #BlackLivesMatter hashtags from celebrity accounts detailed how these particular tweets were more likely to be used for community-building and identity-building rather than simply for marketing products or self-promotion. Thematic analysis of nearly 2.7 million posts identified a number of community-related intentions underpinning #BlackLivesMatter tweets, including what the researchers described as "speaking to whites" – i.e. messages intended to represent the black community to white Twitter audiences. Such uses of Twitter are also noted in "non-celebrity" use of the #BlackLivesMatter hash-tag, with ordinary people rationalizing their use of "black tags" as a means of making sense of discrimination experiences, identifying with their racial group, and contributing to the black community (Lee-Won et al. 2018).

Digital race research has also begun to document the broader phenomenon of "black Twitter" (Sharma 2013). This was initially noted in 2009 in terms of black users' propensity to contribute to "culturally relevant, humorous memes and chats" (Harlow and Benbrook 2018). Yet, in the wake of high-profile racial incidents such as Ferguson, research has increasingly explored the role of Twitter as a site of black activism to contest hegemony and create community.

Indeed, while often engaging in gossip about popular culture, black Twitter users remain more likely than other users to tweet on topics of social justice and politics (Williams 2016). In these ways, researchers have pointed to Twitter functioning as a "meaningful community" (ibid.), a "social public" (Brock 2012) and a "networked counterpublic" (Graham and Smith 2016) for African-American users.

Of course, the collective actions of black Twitter users are mirrored by groups with oppositional racial agendas. Digital race research also contrasts trends such as "black Twitter" with the online actions of pro-white and other racist groups. For example, Nadia Flores-Yeffal and her colleagues (2011, 2018) have addressed the role of the internet in sustaining public discourses in the US surrounding undocumented immigrants – what she terms the "Latino cyber-moral panic." This work explores how blogs, Facebook groups, Twitter and YouTube sustained the contestation of accurate information during the 2010s alongside a continuous circulation of specific phrases (e.g. "overhaul," "wake up," "secure our borders," "make America great again"). Flores-Yeffal argues that these views were then replicated in news media and representations of public opinion and subsequently became part of the dominant public discourse as a "problem" that needs to be solved.

As with all digital sociology research, Flores-Yeffal is careful to disentangle the social and technical dynamics at play in such developments. Drawing on Stanley Cohen's notion of "moral panic," Flores-Yeffal reasons that the internet did not cause people to express these views per se. However, online platforms undoubtedly "exacerbate people's framing of the issue in ways that are then amplified through other media sources" (Flores-Yeffal et al. 2018). Similar conclusions are drawn in Thomas Nakayama's account of the role of the internet in enabling the so-called Birther Movement to sustain the dispute of President Obama's legitimacy as US president on the fictitious grounds of being born in Kenya. As Nakayama (2017: 69) concluded, "despite the traditional mainstream media focus on the legal documents showing that the president was born in Hawaii, the internet enabled the Birther movement to empower its interpretation of President Obama's birthplace."

Digital race – recurring themes and issues

This research and writing powerfully illustrates the racialized ways in which digital media are designed, configured and used, the racialized consequences of these shapings, and the role of digital media as an important "site of political struggle over racial meaning, knowledge and values" (Daniels 2013: 696). In part, this new wave of research is a matter of timing, emanating from a generation of researchers responding to issues that have come to prominence throughout the 2010s. Yet this research is also driven by what was identified in chapters 1 and 2 as the explicitly political focus of digital sociology and its underpinning interests in social relations, social conflict, power and control. In short, all digital researchers clearly need to consider the racialized dimensions of these issues if they want to claim relevance to contemporary digital society. As Jessie Daniels (2016: 337) reasons, "if digital sociology is to prove useful as a field, it must take seriously the ways that racialized and gendered bodies are attacked in and through digital media technologies."

As with this chapter's previous example of digital labor, the immediate question that the digital race literature raises is "what is new here?" Again these studies remind us that "what is new here?" is not a question with a clear-cut answer. This research and writing certainly portrays an increased messiness of racial dynamics in networked, software-based settings. Certainly these studies highlight the foregrounding of certain values and perspectives in the design and implementation of digital platforms and point to ways in which the configuration and governance of digital media continue to be built around an "assumed whiteness" (Kolko 2000: 225). Yet it could be argued that digital media do little more than mirror already established patterns of racial discrimination and oppression. In this respect, platforms such as Twitter, Facebook and Twitch could be seen as merely exposing well-established social relations and dynamics. Indeed, as Tressie Cottom (2016: 217) reasons, it is to be expected that "digitization ... should reproduce unequal social relations of the society that produces it."

Yet the emerging literature on digital race does point to some important differences in the ways that race is being played out through digital platforms, applications and systems. For example, one notable shift appears to be the constrained and disconnected nature of these interactions. The well-noted tendency of social media toward "filter bubbles" and "echo chambers" (Flaxman et al. 2016) means that the production and consumption of racial messages, ideas and understandings is more intense but perhaps not as expansive as they might previously have been. Thus the internet can easily accommodate millions of users vibrantly co-constructing the idea that "Black Lives Matter" while millions of other users blithely work to "Make America Great Again." The logics of digital media ensure that these ostensibly connected groups do not interact meaningfully with each other online, enter dialogue or refine their views.

Indeed, a notable change over the past ten years is the increasingly software-based, programmed constraint of people's interactions with ideas and knowledge. The logic of "platformed racism" certainly appears to be underpinning altered dynamics of racism. Many of these studies suggest that individuals' existing cultural values are directed and intensified in specific ways by the coded structures and politics of commercially produced platforms. Thus, it is not enough to say that online racism arises wholly from the intentions of racist individuals who happen to be using the internet. Instead, digital race research illustrates how structural oppression operates from within the IT industry that produces, provides and governs the digital media being used. Many of the studies just outlined highlight the complicity of platform providers in configuring their products in ways that often appear to exacerbate difference and reduce the possibilities for both nuanced conversation and respectful and open dialogue.

Indeed, much of the research just mentioned highlights the increasing influence of commercial IT industry actors in shaping the racialized dynamics of a nation such as the US. While Facebook, Twitter and Google espouse non-discriminatory values, their services clearly function in ways that reflect "bottom-line" economic imperatives. In this sense, movements such as #BlackLivesMatter can flourish on a platform like Twitter alongside counter-movements such as the pro-police #BlueLivesMatter and the tone-deaf #AllLivesMatter – each of which satisfies the economic imperative of the platform to increase users and volume of content production and circulation (Bock and Figueroa 2018). These are technologies that are shaped by concerns for what is "good for business" rather than any particular ideology or underlying intent. Much of what has just been described might therefore be seen as a consequence of the IT industry's libertarianism and willingness to "imagin[e] a world that's fundamentally without politics" (Turner 2017). Yet, instead of finding a utopian post-racial internet, the studies just outlined emphasize the color-blind racism that results from this approach. Rather than reflecting the actions of racist users, many of the concerns raised in digital race research could be seen as stemming from the position of white privilege and power that pervades the high-tech industry and the Silicon Valley culture.

Conclusions

While highlighting many salient issues specific to the areas of labor and race, these studies also point to a number of broader features of digital sociology as an approach to making sense of contemporary society. This includes a commitment to continually question the newness of "new" technologies. None of these studies conclude that digital technologies are somehow causing change or transforming social relations of their own accord; rather, they are more accurately understood as amplifying, exacerbating, extending and reconfiguring social issues. Crucially, many of these studies suggest that such exacerbations and reconfigurations often appear to take place through the lens of the IT industry and a profit-led technological solutionism which remains morally ambivalent to any imprecisions, inequalities and injustices that may result. Continuing a theme introduced in chapter 2, much of this research also points to the specifically "platformed" nature of contemporary experiences, engagements and encounters. In particular, many of the digital labor and digital race studies outlined in this chapter add to our understandings of the realities of "platform capitalism," especially for the marginalized individuals who work to produce excess value often for minimum reward.

Both these areas of research also illustrate the use of core concepts and social theory in digital sociology. For example, echoing themes from chapter 2, digital labor and digital race are topics that reflect the ambiguous outcomes of increasingly networked ways of being. Moreover, these are both areas of research that make good use of existing social theory, testing and extending ideas from labor process theory and critical race theory. These areas of research also illustrate the diversity of research methods that can be used in the study of digital society. While much can be identified from large-scale computational analyses of 2.7 million tweets, there is in addition much that can be learned from ethnographically "hanging around" with Uber drivers (both online and in their cars). There is also continued value in traditional empirical methods of face-to-face interviewing, observation and documentary analysis. These are research topics that benefit from researchers being as methodologically pluralistic and pragmatic as possible.

Finally, areas such as digital labor and digital race both speak to an underlying concern of digital sociology – i.e. how could things "be otherwise"? For example, in terms of digital labor research, a number of convincing arguments have emerged with regard to the need to reimagine and reconstitute the notion of organized labor and trade unionism for the digital age – what Walker (2012: 39) describes as "a high-tech labor movement." Elsewhere are suggestions for the establishment of alternative online platforms that function as worker cooperatives rather than as for-profit entities (Scholz 2016). Similarly, digital race research is proving a useful basis from which to imagine alternative forms of digital media and internet use. For example, in terms of education, Tanksley (2016) advances the idea of a "black feminist media literacy" that supports the development of skills to analyze media codes and speak back to or criticize dominant ideologies in digital media. Other suggestions include the development of alternative digital technologies – for example, interfaces, algorithms and other key mediating artifacts that are accommodating to (rather than dominating of) racial identities other than white (see Cheney-Lippold 2017).

All told, the burgeoning literatures around digital labor and digital race offer rich illustrations of digital sociology in practice. Extending this theme, the next two chapters reflect further on the practice of digital sociology research and scholarship. What are the methodological concerns that underpin studies such as those reviewed in this chapter? What do these researchers subsequently "do" with their writing and research in terms of making a contribution to the ongoing shaping of digital society? In the first instance, chapter 4 goes on to consider the methodology and methods of digital sociology research. Just how should we set about doing digital sociology research?

4
Digital Methods and Methodology

Introduction

The studies featured in chapter 3 illustrate an increasingly diverse use of research tools and techniques in digital sociology. Only a few years on from anticipation of a "new kind of social science" (Christakis 2012), digital sociologists are now engaged in all manner of innovative empirical methods and approaches. While remaining conscious of the limitations and compromises inherent in any empirical endeavor, digital sociologists are certainly thinking expansively and imaginatively about how they research, as well as about what they research.

The sense of methodological reinvention resonates with ongoing concerns across the discipline over the "fitness for purpose" of social research. Well before talk of a digital sociology, Savage and Burrows's (2007) "The coming crisis of empirical sociology" forewarned of the declining prominence and purpose of twentieth-century social sciences. Here it was contended that the authority of sociology, cultural studies and political sciences was fast fading in light of research innovations outside the academy that far exceeded the scale and scope of data generated through academic research. In particular, Burrows and Savage (2014) noted that corporations, government agencies and other "commercial sociology" actors are now utilizing digitally generated data with the promise of yielding comprehensive evidence of genuine actions.

Against this background, favored sociological methods such as the individual in-depth interview certainly appear rather paltry and under-powered in contrast to millions of users routinely reflecting their life-worlds and world-views through social media. "Big picture" data such as this, Savage and Burrows (2007: 885) reasoned, fundamentally undermines any claim that sociologists might have had previously to privileged or especially insightful "access to the social." Patricia Clough and her colleagues (2015: 147) have elsewhere referred to this as "the datalogical turn," where "large-scale databases and adaptive algorithms are calling forth a new onto-logic of sociality or the social itself." Mass quantities of digital data certainly constitute a significant challenge to sociology – offering a competing framework that promises to make sense of the social world on a far more expansive, comprehensive and rapid basis.

The empirical ambitions of digital sociology therefore fit alongside various like-minded attempts to rediscover the purpose and verve of sociological research. One such example is the manifesto for "live methods" of Les Back and his colleagues (Back 2012), which stresses the need for research infused with a spirit "alive to the processes by which society is made" (Michael 2012: 166). This description of live methods foregrounds inquiry that is in "real time" and constantly on the move with people and their practices. It suggests research approaches that are artful, creative, playful and deliberately provocative – pushing sociological researchers to develop empirical methods and "probes" that test and reinvent relations with social settings and environments. As the live methods movement reminds us, digital sociology is certainly not alone in looking to move beyond the traditional "qualitative vs. quantitative" concerns of the discipline.

Yet digital sociology has particular reason to look beyond the habitual use of social research methods past their prime. In short, digital sociologists are pursuing research interests that cannot be reflected or captured solely through interviews and sample surveys. As the past three chapters have established, digital sociology research addresses vast socio-technical assemblages of human users and devices overlaid by all manner of software, data and algorithms. These are topics of research that demand methods that are "technology-centric," "data-centric" *and* "social-centric" (Marres 2017). As Marres continues, digital sociology research demands the combination of "external" approaches that address digital technology through the lens of sociality and society with "internal" approaches that address the social through the lens of digital architecture. As we shall now go on to discuss, current digital sociology research pursues this balance through a number of distinct methodological approaches.

Big Data and the computational social sciences

One key methodological concern for digital sociologists is so-called Big Data. While it is an overused term, Big Data signals an immensely expanded scale and scope of research, alongside heightened expectations of the social insights this can yield. In a basic sense, Big Data refers to computerized processing of massive sets of digital information. This takes place through automated archiving and tagging, linking and connecting, harvesting and mining of data through various computer-based processes. With the ever-increasing computational capacity of digital systems allowing such processes to take place on a mass aggregated scale, even modestly resourced individual researchers can now work with huge amounts of data to discover patterns that would otherwise be imperceptible (Boyd and Crawford 2012).

Big Data methods are well established throughout the natural sciences (e.g. genetics, environmental science and astronomy) as well as in business and government sectors. With increasing amounts of data relating to social domains being produced, sociological researchers have growing opportunities to follow suit. Indeed, massive quantities of social digital data now originate from a variety of different sources in a number of different forms. Large amounts of social data are generated deliberately. This includes the administrative measurement of people's interactions with government agencies and commercial interests, as well as more covert forms of institutional monitoring and evaluation of individuals. At the same time, vast quantities of data are generated through the operations of digital devices and systems. Moreover, people volunteer large volumes of data during the course of their use of digital technologies, in particular the curation of social media profiles and various other forms of user-generated content.

This all amounts to what has been described as an (over) abundance of "big and broad" social data (Housley et al. 2014) offering a ready means of addressing social science questions. The hype surrounding social uses of Big Data is considerable – often framed along lines of a "new way of knowing society" (Marres 2017: 17) that offers "to reveal the reality of human behavior at scale" (Carrigan 2015). The idea of Big Data certainly raises advantages in comparison to traditional sources of sociological data. Computational methods allow for considerably more data to be processed than would be possible manually, with "extended zoomability between micro and macro" (Evans and Rees 2012: 23). Most Big Data sets are updated regularly, thereby facilitating real-time (rather than snapshot) analysis over finite periods of weeks and months. This can support ongoing bottom-up inductions of social activity which reveal patterns and structures as they occur (rather than analyses based on *a priori* interests of the researcher).

The promise of Big Data certainly chimes with the interests of many sociologists. After all, detecting patterns among unstructured information is a central element of sociological research (Hannigan 2015). Of course, most sociologists are understandably circumspect about excessive claims of Big Data offering an all-seeing analytic eye. Yet, such hyperbole notwithstanding, Big Data has emboldened those sociologists who see themselves pursuing "analytic" work rather than "critique" (Williams et al. 2017). From this perspective, Big Data has been welcomed as a "watershed moment" (McFarland et al. 2016) that redresses the "imbalance of theory and data" hitherto characterizing many areas of sociology (Bail 2014: 476). Big Data might not "know everything," but there is growing belief that it dramatically increases researchers' insights into the social.

Interest in Big Data brings digital sociology into the realms of what has come to be known as the "computational social sciences." This "interdisciplinary renaissance" (Hannigan 2015: 5) sees social science questions being tackled through techniques developed within the data sciences. In an early call to arms, Lazer and his colleagues proposed that computational social science techniques could support ambitious sociological analyses, such as "what a 'macro' social network of society looks like" (Lazer et al. 2009: 722). Key techniques involve various means of data mining, modeling and mapping large-scale data-sets to support the simulation and analysis of social phenomena. In contrast to sociology's traditional preference for written text and (on occasion) numbers, computational social science approaches make extensive use of visual-based interpretations. All of this leaves Big Data methods appearing distinctly exotic in comparison to most other areas of sociological research.

Sociologists are making use of Big Data approaches in a number of ways. Alongside a resurgence of large-scale social network analysis, one particular area of interest is "topic modeling" from large corpora of textual data. As DiMaggio et al. (2013: 570) reason, the adoption of this approach from computer science and natural language processing addresses a long-standing methodological "puzzle" for sociologists faced with large quantities of textual data – i.e. "how can researchers ... capture the information we need, reduce its complexity, and provide interpretations that are substantively plausible and statistically validated?" Topic modeling does this by using algorithms to identify statistically proximate clusters of words (latent topics) that an analyst can then match to their knowledge of the field. By focusing on the co-occurrence of words, the technique offers a powerful means of highlighting contextual meanings, frames and symbolic boundaries of the patterns that are identified (Mützel 2015). Recent studies using this approach have explored everything from the prevalence of economic topics in the academic sociological literature to the public discourse surrounding Facebook's attempt to implement its "Free Basics" internet service in India (Shahin 2018). Big Data approaches allow these issues to be addressed at scale rather than on the basis of a few hundred texts. For example, Daoud and Kohl's (2016) study of economic sociology was based on analysis of 140,000 academic articles in 157 different journals between 1890 and 2014.

Perhaps the most popular forms of Big Data analyses involve examining outputs from Twitter, Instagram and other social media, which are appealing to sociologists for a number of reasons. These are mass archives of text, images and interactions between hundreds of millions of individuals. Moreover, these platforms are already configured to elicit sociological information from users – detailing networks of "friends," what people "like" and how they are feeling. Furthermore, from a technical point of view, platforms such as Twitter make data publicly available and provide APIs (application programming interfaces) that allow data to be easily extracted and reused. Academic journals now feature a growing number of social media Big Data studies which tend to analyze large corpora of posts by means of keyword tracking and sentiment analysis – examining how information is shared, alongside what emotions are expressed and opinions formed. The scale of these studies is often vast – for example, investigations of more than 60 million tweets relating to Occupy movements around the US (Agarwal et al. 2014) or nearly 4.6 billion tweets pertaining to public events over a 33-month period (Dodds et al. 2011). While many of these analyses are retrospective, some studies seek to analyze data on a real-time basis, supporting forms of "social listening" (Hollander and Hartt 2017) and even predictive forms of "social forecasting" and "social sensing" (Williams et al. 2017).

Notable early studies focused on social media activity that surrounded social movements such as Occupy, the Arab Spring and various instances of civil unrest and disorder around the world (see Bruns et al. 2013; Agarwal et al. 2014; Hoofd 2014). Other prominent areas of study include public discourse around national election campaigns and the sharing of images and videos in the aftermath of terror attacks in Europe (Williams and Burnap 2015; Bruns and Hanusch 2017). These latter studies seek to identify forms of "connective witnessing" and sense-making, exploring emotive as well as fact-sharing aspects of the responses. When replicated, such investigations allow for the tracking over time of significant societal shifts. As we saw in chapter 3, for example, studies of public reaction to repeated US race-related incidents offer a powerful picture of the dynamics underpinning the still developing "national conversation on racism" (Houghton et al. 2018).

While such approaches have been well received and frequently cited, significant tensions have emerged between the promise and practicalities of Big Data analysis. These are incredibly complex procedures, and, while many sociologists remain wary of excessive claims of a new form of "forensic social science" (McFarland et al. 2016), it is easy to overlook the incomplete and inconsistent nature of such processes. Thus some observers are keen to stress that Big Data (and its analysis) needs to be seen as a contestable process, "often unreliable, prone to outages and losses" (Boyd and Crawford 2012: 668). Indeed, an obvious point to make from a sociological perspective is that these processes of meaning-making are never wholly neutral, objective and "automated" but are fraught with problems and compromises, biases and omissions. Thus, as with all forms of data generation, some of the key challenges to "big social data" relate to representation (with finite sets of characteristics being decided to "count" as a particular entity) and reductionism (with artificially neat boundaries and categories being drawn around data). These concerns extend into data analysis processes, with analysts invariably having to further clean up data-sets in order to render then "algorithm ready" (Mützel 2015), yet in the process inducing further omissions and simplifications. This also relates to concern over "machine bias" (Marres 2017: 120) and how analyses are shaped by the specific digital tools being used. For example, the predominance of studies favoring Twitter reflects the fact that Twitter makes data more readily available to researchers than platforms such as Facebook. Similarly, a researcher's choice of API to "scrape" data has been shown to generate substantially different results. Even before any interpretation takes place, it is important to acknowledge that these are not neutral data-sets and analytic tools which lead to objective results.

Perhaps the most serious limitation of Big Data is the issue of context. As Bail (2014: 477) concedes, "the most vexing problem is that Big Data often does not include information about the social context in which texts are produced." For example, while the large-scale Trisma data project involving 3.7 million Australian Twitter accounts was able to identify a "major spike" in Twitter signups coinciding with a devastating earthquake in Nepal, the researchers were forced to concede that "we've yet to determine why that event would lead to new Twitter accounts being created in Australia" (Bruns 2017). Concerns therefore remain over the descriptive nature of these analyses. As with all secondary data analysis, researchers inevitably suffer a "loss of control" over research design when using Big Data sets (Housley et al. 2014), limited in what can be achieved by the nature and form of the data at their disposal. Thus, it is increasingly suggested that this results in studies that offer little more than data exploration rather than data analysis. As Rieder and Röhle (2012: 70) put it, "while their results may be visually impressive and intuitively convincing, the methodological and epistemological status of their output seems unclear at best."

"Thick data" and the digital ethnographic turn

These latter concerns reflect a notable pushback against Big Data. While it would be misleading to talk of a methodological schism, growing numbers of digital sociologists are now questioning what is being lost in the turn toward the computational social sciences. Thus, while its stock might continue to rise in other disciplines, "the big data paradigm appears to have become somewhat becalmed" in terms of academic sociology (Halford and Savage 2017: 1139). Growing numbers of sociologists, it seems, have become suspicious of "the epistemological chutzpah of big data" (McFall and Deville 2017: 127).

In particular, while computational social science research can certainly lay claim to being "big," its application of "data" in a sociological sense is less convincing. As Venturini and Latour (2010) contend, the sociological idea of "data" infers some connection to context and setting, with sufficient meaning to allow the extraction of information. Instead Big Data – especially when derived from digital devices and platforms – is perhaps more accurately described as "traces." These traces are often linked to little more than an individual's "doings" (such as physical movements) and specific actions (such as transactions, choices, statements, interactions) (Ruppert et al. 2013). Thus the data that constitutes Big Data could reasonably be criticized as often "lacking in demographic detail" (Halford and Savage 2017) and other forms of sociologically "useful knowledge" (Venturini et al. 2017).

These suspicions are bolstered by growing acknowledgment of how the traces that constitute Big Data sets are shaped substantively by the digital devices and platforms by which they are produced. For example, a corpus of tweets represents a distinct form of communication – limited to 280 characters and shaped by protocols of hash-tags, sub-tweeting, "likes," and so on. In this sense, Twitter "conversations" are not natural speech acts but are structured and scripted by the platforms that facilitate their generation. Any conclusions drawn from a study of 4.6 billion tweets therefore carries the proviso that social media "perform and produce sociality as much as they describe it" (Burrows and Savage 2014: 5).

With these criticisms in mind, there is growing interest in contrasting the notion of "big and broad" social data with research that strives for specificity and granularity in the form of "small and deep" data. In particular, this has seen a notable resurgence of enthusiasm within digital sociology toward ethnographic sensibilities and approaches as a means of harnessing "the descriptive power of the social sciences" (Burrows and Savage 2014: 3). In contrast to Big Data, digitally related forms of ethnography suggest the use of a wide range of evidence sources to support the building of rich narrative and critical reflection. In this sense, it is reasoned that ethnographic studies of digital settings "can act as a contextual counter-balance" (Barrett and Maddox 2016: 703) to the computational social sciences through the generation of "thick data" with depth and meaning. As Tricia Wang (2013) describes, "Thick Data is data brought to light using qualitative, ethnographic research methods that uncover people's emotions, stories, and models of their world ... Thick Data can rescue Big Data from the context-loss that comes with the processes of making it usable."

One strand of this "thick" approach consists of so-called trace methods. These take inspiration from the STS notion of charting the journeys of objects, following how digital "things" move around and through coded architectures and networks. Such studies continue the tradition of "ethnography of infrastructure" (e.g. Star 1999), albeit with the distinction that these are investigations of coded rather than material structures. For example, "trace ethnography" of digital data (Geiger and Ribes 2011) focuses on the detailed traces generated and collated by online systems. These include transaction logs, version histories, institutional records, conversation transcripts and source code. Observation of how these various forms of data are (re)constituted and (re)circulated within digital systems can yield rich insights into online practices, collaborations and coordinations within the groups and organizations using them.

One example of this approach are trace studies of Wikipedia editing and administration, such as Geiger and Ribes's (2011) study of Wikipedia article deletion and Weltevrede and Borra's (2016) tracing of "processes of dispute" within Wikipedia's edit history and talk page functions. As Geiger and Ribes (2011: 1) observe:

> Analysis of these detailed and heterogeneous data ... can provide rich qualitative insight into the interactions of users, allowing us to retroactively reconstruct specific actions at a fine level of granularity. Once decoded, sets of such documentary traces can then be assembled into rich narratives of interaction, allowing researchers to carefully follow coordination practices, information flows, situated routines, and other social and organizational phenomena across a variety of scales.

This emphasis on software-based inquiry is also reflected in the continuing production of ethnographies of online communities situated wholly "in the network" (Lane 2016: 47). One of the best known of these studies is Tom Boellstorff's (2008) ethnography of the popular 2000s virtual world "Second Life." This study took place wholly online, reflecting Boellstorff's (2008: 60) commitment to researching online settings "in their own terms." Approaching Second Life in this manner led to detailed descriptions of inhabitants' enactment of online forms of intimacy and community alongside the development of shared understandings of place, time and "virtual person-hood." The study also produced rich descriptions of the dominant forms of governance, surveillance and resistance within the virtual world. All told, Boellstorff produced accounts of Second Life that were as detailed as he might have produced of any face-to-face community or locality. Such studies therefore shine a valuable light on logics and practices of digital culture that other approaches underrepresent or overlook altogether. This is evident, for example, in recent ethnographic studies of the "dark web" (Gehl 2016) and communities of drug users using anonymous dark-web "cyptomarkets" (Barratt and Maddox 2016). It is hard to imagine how else these significant (albeit unfamiliar and under-reported) aspects of digital culture might otherwise be studied.

Alongside these fully "online" ethnographies are studies that combine digitally mediated descriptions with data generated through face-to-face encounters. The past ten years have seen a proliferation of such ethnographies, covering topics such as teenagers' everyday uses of digital media (Takahashi 2014), the working practices of software developers (Seaver 2017), and the establishment of community wireless networks in rapidly gentrifying urban areas (Cardullio 2017). While many of these studies are focused primarily on digital issues and topics, this growth also reflects acknowledgment among traditional on-the-ground ethnographers of the need to delve into the digital. For example, Jeffrey Lane's ethnographic study of street life in a Harlem neighborhood illustrates the ways in which the researcher quickly realized that "social life on the street unfolds in person and through social media" (Lane 2016: 43). As Lane continues, "my observations on the sidewalk were insufficient without the relevant digital data. The digital data alone would also have been inadequate ... street life is characterized by its flow online and offline. As ethnographers, we have to keep up" (ibid.: 44)

Running throughout these studies is an interest in people's lived experiences of the digital. This is research that seeks to explore the multiple ways that the digital is encountered, the emergence of digital practices, and the cultural logics and shared understandings that develop around digital forms. One particular strength of this research is developing understandings of how people come into contact with the digital.

As noted in chapter 2, approaching the digital in terms of human experience is a key concern of digital sociology, yet this is an understandably tricky aspect to research. As Sarah Pink and her colleagues (2016: 16) reason, "experience is ultimately unique to individuals. We cannot actually access other people's experiences in any direct way." Thus while still relying on classic ethnographic methods of being-in-place, observing, talking, and generally hanging around, digital ethnography is increasingly exploring the empirical study of the sensually rich and varied nature of technology use. For example, using digital video, geolocation data and touch-responsive technologies, ethnographers are exploring how digital media are experienced through all senses. This therefore encompasses the bodily movements that take place around digital technologies, the three-dimensional shaping and textures of digital devices, the beeps, clicks, whirrs and other noises of technology, and even the heat and smells generated by devices.

All of the studies just outlined illustrate the value of ethnographic approaches in accounting for the digital. Most of these studies retain a fundamental essence of traditional ethnographic work, describing digital technology use as messy, performed, taking symbolic and material forms, and being locally enacted. In continuing these long-standing points of concern, digital ethnography offers a useful way "to understand the digital as part of something wider, rather than situating it at the center of our work" (Pink et al. 2016: 11). That said, all these studies involve the modification and refinement of traditional ethnographic practices. As Hine (2015: 6) puts it, this is "ethnography adapted for the circumstances that the contemporary internet provides." Hine distinguishes this as developing an ethnography "for" the internet, in contrast to ethnography "of" or "through" the internet.

Coding, programming and software development

Alongside Big Data and digital ethnographies is a burgeoning trend of research based around the design, development and implementation of software and coded artifacts. This approach chimes with a number of methodological ideas, not least Richard Rogers's notion of "natively digital" research, where he argues for repurposing the techniques and protocols of digital objects in the service of social research. As Rogers (2013: 1) puts it, this involves "thinking along with" (rather than thinking against) the digital devices and digital objects being studied. This can involve either repurposing digital media in ways that make them productive sources of social research data or even creating new code and software from scratch.

Such research also echoes Noortje Marres's notion of "approaching the digital *from the inside out*" – i.e. making use of methods that are "embedded in digital infrastructures and practices" (Marres 2017: 84, emphasis in original). However, some of the most generative examples of this approach occur when researchers are responsible themselves for embedding these methods into digital media. In this sense, clear parallels can be drawn with the idea of live methods, in particular the notion of playful and sometimes obtuse ways of doing research through the creation of artifacts and objects. All told, then, this is research that responds directly to the challenge that, "in relation to digital devices ..., we need to get our hands dirty" (Ruppert et al. 2013: 32).

There are a number of studies that reflect these aspirations. First is what Benjamin Haber (2016: 153) describes as code-based "active experimentation with the forms and formulas of digital media." Such an approach fits with recent thinking elsewhere in sociology and beyond. For example, there has of late been an uptake of experimental and interventionist research designs across many areas of sociology, as well as a rise of programming-based interventions in the humanities areas of "critical code studies" and "software studies" (e.g. Fuller 2008). In common with these areas, the driving impetus for digital sociology is to engage in design and implementation of software that is likely to push boundaries and test the limits of coded environments.

Interesting applications of this "build it yourself" approach include Birkbak and Carlsen's (2016) experimental analyses of the algorithms deployed by platforms such as Facebook,

Twitter and Google. Elsewhere, cultural geographers in the niche area of "drone methods" have been involved in piloting drones into unauthorized areas to test the material and coded parameters of data-based "geo-fencing" (Fish et al. 2017). Also of note is the use by Murthy and his colleagues (2016) of Twitter "bots" to explore the nature of public discourse during the 2015 UK general election. This latter study saw the researchers developing a series of "social bots" – algorithmically controlled Twitter accounts that are programmed to attempt to appear human. Social bots can either directly control their own accounts and create new content autonomously or else relay and repurpose messages from other pre-existing accounts. The researchers asked human volunteers to tweet using hash-tags from purpose-made Twitter accounts during key televised events in the election process. Bots were linked to the accounts of some participants, while other accounts remained untouched. This allowed the researchers to monitor how online political communication was influenced by autonomous as well as human interactions. These activities produced a series of temporal network graphs showing the development and diversification of the "bot-influenced" and "bot-free" online discussions.

Another strand of work has emerged from research in the emerging area of "critical data studies." One line of inquiry here is to explore processes of making "personal data" and the machinations of the commercial data-brokering industry more accessible to ordinary users (Kennedy and Moss 2015). Research by Skeggs and Yuill (2016) pursued this by combining information gleaned from Facebook's own official API with their own bespoke developed plug-in tool that was designed to extract data relating to participants' Facebook activity that was otherwise not available from the API. This plug-in revealed the advertising shown to users on Facebook, as well as indicating how Facebook was tracking users as they browsed elsewhere. This information was then used by participants to reflect on their engagements with Facebook – allowing the researchers to "open up the black box" of the platform, if only temporarily.

Other studies have worked with young social media users to co-create software tools to gain a similar sense of their personal data generation and its reuse by third parties such as advertisers and data brokers. Pybus et al. (2015) augmented the development of their "MobileMiner" plug-in with a series of hackathons to support participants' understandings of the personal data that was being generated and reused. Similarly, Selwyn and Pangrazio's (2018) "PDQ" smartphone app was co-created with young people to give participants insight into how their personal data was processed by industry-standard data analytics and profiling tools (in the form of three commercial APIs concerned with facial recognition, sentiment analysis and geolocation data). The focus of both these projects on repurposing APIs was deliberate. As Pybus et al. (2015: 4) reasoned, "if a user does not understand how they can leverage their API, nor understand its technical constraints, then they are unable to effectively interact with the platform."

Another strand of this approach is perhaps more obtrusive and bordering on absurdist. This work follows the live methods ethos of developing and letting loose "cultural probes" that test and reinvent relations with social settings and environments. Particularly noteworthy is Mike Michael's (2012) encouragement of "idiotic" methods, such as the "speculative design" of provocative objects and probes that might disrupt or misbehave in social settings. Indeed, Michael has pursued this approach in research involving the programming of nonsensical automated Twitter bots. In one study, researchers sought to explore the dynamics of Twitter-based discussions of energy reduction (Wilkie et al. 2015), testing the limits of what might be constitute acceptable actors, communities and practices. They developed and implemented three distinct social bots designed to respond earnestly, unpredictably or nonsensically to other users' messages that they calculated to be related to energy reduction topics. These coded incursions provoked many Twitter users to engage with the bots and therefore expose and test the constitution and dynamics of the community of Twitter accounts engaged in the area. As the researchers put it, this study used these coded interventions to "make visible the emergent actors, collectives and communities" on Twitter (ibid.: 90).

A similar approach was taken by Bayne (2015) in her development of a deliberately "dumb" teaching Twitter bot for a university online master's course with over 12,000 students. This coded experiment was intended to probe pedagogically generative instances where students encountered what they presumed to be a knowledgeable tutor, but soon realized this was not the case. Instead, the bot was programmed to return a series of pre-prepared statements, questions and provocations which were triggered by particular keywords as they appeared in students' course-related tweets. These researchers were interested in exploring the micro-level interactional implications of education delivered along AI-based, "post-human" lines. The study's use of what many students quickly came to befriend as "Botty" provided a speculative means of addressing these issues.

These latter provocative and contrary research approaches certainly offer an alternative to the grand, authoritative sensibility of the computational social sciences. These are interventions that are intrusive, annoying and antagonistic, yet serve an important purpose in unpacking the human/code entanglements that constitute all digital practices and environments. It could be argued that such "device-driven" (rather than "data-driven") perspectives on digital research direct attention toward "the operational capacities of digital media" (Weltevrede 2016: 2). Certainly, many of the examples just mentioned act to repurpose digital tools away from (and even against) commercial logics and imperatives of dominant platforms. Indeed, it is reasoned that these approaches are valuable in generating what has been termed thick data (as opposed to Big Data) that "trace the articulations of technical, corporate and media logics" (Langlois and Elmer 2013: 2). As Skeggs and Yuill (2016: 1368) concluded of their critical incursions into Facebook:

> We did "get inside" one example of capital's new lines of flight. Our understandings of lifeness and rhythms, via software and methods that visualized networks, interfaces, entanglements, algorithms, encounters, person/a/s, conductivity, platformativity, time, tone, transduction and lifeness, hopefully open out ways of understanding some of the ways by which Facebook works. ... It is a small sample of big data, designed not to just describe patterns and networks, but also temporal rhythms, attention and activity beyond and through the interface.

Looking to the future of digital sociological methods

Rather than facing a methodological crisis, it could be contended that digital sociology is emerging during a time of methodological opportunity. As this chapter has illustrated, digital sociologists have license to be flexible and eclectic in their appropriation of methods. If there is a common methodological approach to digital sociology, then it might perhaps best be described as a broad spirit of adventure rather than as a narrowly prescriptive set of rules and tools. In particular, digital sociologists are becoming increasingly confident in appropriating the digital aspects of what is being researched as potential tools (as well as objects) of study. As Ruppert (2013: 273) puts it, this is an area of sociology that demands the use of methods that are "more in and of" digital worlds – "not standing outside and detached from them as objects or subjects of inquiry."

As the examples in this chapter suggest, this involves being mindful of the forms of inquiry that might be inscribed within the devices, platforms and systems that we are researching – taking advantage of what Marres (2017: 103) terms "the methods of the medium" to engage in "a critique from within" (Ruppert 2013: 273). Sometimes this might call for being creative, playful and pragmatic, as can be seen in the act of repurposing (or even mis-purposing) digital media for social research purposes (Rogers 2013). Yet, for every instance of letting a few "idiotic" social bots loose on Twitter and seeing what happens, digital sociology is also home to studies that engage carefully and sensitively with collections of 4.6 million tweets. Digital sociology research can be broad and diverse in its approaches.

Indeed, alongside these developments it is important to recognize the importance of retaining and revitalizing traditional methods of research. As Marres (2017: 38) reflects, "we must not fall into the trap of "overstat[ing] the newness of digital sociology." Many digital sociology studies continue to make good use of interviews, observations, visual methods and documentary approaches in researching digital contexts. Much can continue to be gained from working with older sociological methods and methodological traditions, particularly as a respite from the relentless churn of digital systems and real-time data streams. Indeed, an undoubted benefit of "old-fashioned" interviews, observations and sample surveys is their capacity to force even the most hurried researcher or participant to slow down, take stock and pause for thought. Simply sitting down with interviewees face to face while "scrolling back" through their Facebook timelines can be a surprisingly effective method of inquiry (Robards and Lincoln 2017). However lively in intent, social research always benefits from taking one's time and thinking carefully.

Thus most digital sociologists remain open to using any type of method that offers them insights into the digital. Rather than sticking blindly to a limited and approved repertoire, digital sociologists are in the enviable position of being encouraged (if not expected) to take methods from software studies, computer sciences and data sciences and "adjust them to serve sociological purposes" (Marres 2017: 81). This does not mean grabbing hold of novel methods and techniques "simply because they are easy to use" (ibid.: 112). Instead, it means making appropriate use of the insights offered by "technology-centric," "data-centric" and "social-centric" approaches.

Of course, this entails a range of skills and competencies that might well lie outside the "comfort zone" of many sociologists (Zook et al. 2017: 1). Thus it is important that they gain a good grasp of the technological underpinnings of the new methods they are deploying. Anyone looking to enter digital sociology would do well to develop a working knowledge of data structures and algorithms, alongside skills in coding, programming and statistics. Digital sociologists also need to be skilled in terms of data visualization. This is not to say that we should all enroll for computer science degrees. Yet it is helpful at least to be able to have informed conversations about these tools we are "using" (or, more accurately, that are being "used" in our research). Another key area of development relates to ethical understandings of these methods. Having access to swathes of Big Data does not absolve researchers from the usual ethical standards expected from academic research – after all, it needs to be remembered that most Big Data "represent or impact people" (Zook et al. 2017).

Similarly, being "playful" does not diminish researchers' ethical responsibilities. Many sociologists were quick to condemn Facebook's "emotional contagion" experiments (conducted with psychologists from Princeton) that altered the newsfeeds of 689,000 Facebook users (Kramer et al. 2014). Yet how does this compare with the research ethics of introducing disruptive social bots into Twitter conversations and communities? The ethics of digital research are increasingly complex and contentious.

As these latter points imply, such methods do not require that digital sociologists simply develop technical skills. More important, perhaps, is developing understandings of these methods and "tuning in" to the sensibilities of these approaches and what they can do. This includes the ability to anticipate issues that are capable of being raised by the data being generated and therefore formulating appropriate questions. In terms of Big Data, for example, this is seen to involve viewing the social world on a considerably different scale from that which sociologists might otherwise be accustomed (Mann 2012). Thus, perhaps the biggest challenges raised by these methods are ontological. As Burrows and Savage (2014: 3) put it, the scope and scale of what these digital methods can tell us about social life "might demand nothing less than a fundamental re-description of what it is that needs to be explained and understood by the social sciences."

So to what extent does capacity exist within the sociological workforce to rise to these challenges? If capacity is lacking, then to what extent are these methods inherently interdisciplinary and demanding that sociologists collaborate with computational disciplines? For sure, the skilled labor of programming APIs, scraping data-sets and developing apps calls for expertise in the computer sciences and data sciences. What was referred to earlier as "build it yourself" is usually more practically a case of "get it built by somebody else." Even developing a simple app or plug-in is a complex, elongated technical process. Ideally, then, digital sociology is not something that can be conducted by lone sociologists. At the moment these are methods that are most successfully deployed through combinations of "computationally literate social scientists and socially literate computer scientists" (Lazer et al. 2009: 722).

The interesting question raised here, then, is whether such work might best be conducted by a new breed of trans-disciplinary "computational social scientists" – i.e. newly formed experts in the combination of both approaches. There are certainly moves afoot in many universities to train and nurture students along these lines. Yet the experiences of those already involved in interdisciplinary teams suggest that perhaps the most fruitful approach might remain collaborations between expert sociologists working alongside expert computer scientists. As Venturini et al. (2017: 3) reflected after ten years working in the "médialab" at Sciences Po in Paris, "engineers, computer scientists, developers and data geeks know how to nurture this kind of data in ways that social scientists still have to learn."

Thus, perhaps digital sociologists are best advised to get involved enthusiastically in these methodological advances while also retaining a detached critical sociological eye over proceedings. While developments such as Big Data certainly "challenge the praxis of doing sociology" (Mützel 2015: 3), this does not mean that sociologists need feel that they are placed on the back foot. Instead, digital sociology is already playing an important role in pushing back – questioning, challenging and subverting these methods in ways that best fit the interests and purposes of the discipline. All told, digital sociology can play a leading role in developing a compelling case for the need for sociological research in a digital age – as Burrows and Savage (2014: 3) put it, "to reinvigorate a sociological imagination ... in ways that could claim back a distinctive jurisdiction over the study of the social."

Conclusions

In times when sociological research faces a number of challenges (if perhaps not full-blown crises), digital sociology certainly offers an intriguing set of possibilities. This chapter has outlined a number of ways that digital sociology allows researchers to move beyond the usual social methods "toolbox." There is plenty of scope for the imaginative and ambitious use of Big Data, digital ethnography, and critical coding approaches. Yet, while these methods provide a useful space for sociologists to establish interdisciplinary approaches and collaborations with computational disciplines, we should not lose sight of the need to adopt and adapt such approaches in an appropriately sociological manner. Digital sociology is not simply a call for sociological researchers to reorientate themselves unthinkingly as data scientists, computer programmers and developers.

Indeed, digital sociology should perhaps be seen as a prompt for sociologists to augment and broaden their skills and competencies rather than narrow and displace them. In this spirit, we can now move on to the final chapter. This addresses the most practical of the four strands of the digital sociology project – i.e. implications of the digital for how we "do" sociology. This relates to the ways in which digital technologies and digital sensibilities are implicated in an expanded notion of sociological craft, scholarship and practice. So, what is the impact of digital technologies on the ways that sociologists are now able to work – particularly in terms of sharing content and engaging with others in more open and collaborative ways? What does it mean to be a digital sociologist in an age of online engagement and "impact"? How can we become genuine "digital scholars" while still remaining scholarly in what we do?

5
Being a Digital Sociologist

Introduction

For many readers, perhaps the most familiar aspect of digital sociology will be its implications for how sociology is "done." This final chapter reflects on the craft, scholarship and practice of digital sociology. In particular, it considers the close alignment between digital sociology and what has been described as "digital scholarship" (Weller 2011) and "networked participatory scholarship" (Veletsianos and Kimmons 2012). These labels convey the idea that academics now operate as "digitized knowledge workers" (Lupton 2014: 66) – i.e. working in ways that are inherently social, accelerated and openly connected with others.

Martin Weller (2011) – an early proponent of digital scholarship – points to three distinct shifts in digital practice that he sees as reshaping contemporary academic work. This entails (i) the diverse nature of the digital content that scholars now find themselves producing and consuming, (ii) the growing significance of social networks in academic work, and (iii) the "open" models of interaction and access inherent in working online. These characteristics differ significantly from twentieth-century scholarly practices, which were shaped by the analogue systems within which they took place. Weller contends that academic libraries, print-based publishing, face-to-face conferences, seminars and courses are all systems built upon the premise of maintaining high thresholds to accessing knowledge. In contrast, networked digital technologies can now support scholarly practices that are far less bounded. Key here are practices of "openness" and "sharing," which Weller (2011: 7) sees as technical features of new digital technologies as well as a "state of mind" for the people who are using them. So, if we accept that these shifts are now prevalent in academic practice, what does this mean for sociologists? Most importantly, in what ways is digital sociology entwined with these forms of scholarship?

The diverse nature of digital sociology practitioners

There is certainly an openness regarding who is engaged in digital sociology. As evident throughout this book, digital sociology involves scholars from a broad range of backgrounds. For example, as highlighted in chapter 4, digital sociology is an increasingly collaborative, interdisciplinary venture between social sciences, humanities, and computational and data sciences. Tellingly, many of the social scientists whose research comes under the aegis of digital sociology would consider themselves working firmly outside of "sociology." As was noted in chapter 2, some of the most sophisticated sociological questions of technology are being asked by academics who would describe themselves as urban geographers, critical data scholars, social media researchers, and so on. Digital sociology is not a field that fits easily into traditional notions of what "sociology" is.

This cross-disciplinary nature reflects the status of digital sociology as a "born digital" field of study. People are finding digital sociology to be an appealing base from which to work because of its development primarily in online environments rather than physical university departments. Regardless of an individual's immediate circumstances and contacts, the #Digital-Sociology hash-tag and similar ports of call provide an invaluable "virtual staffroom" and supporting "collegial solidarity" for anyone interested in these issues (Lupton et al. 2017: 12). Unlike their colleagues in some other areas of sociology, digital sociologists are less concerned with your sociological clique or the institution where you happen to be employed.

This characteristic of digital sociology as a free-floating field has proven especially significant for those researchers and writers employed in precarious quasi-academic jobs – what has become termed the "alt-ac" (alternative academic) workforce. Perhaps more than most other areas of the social sciences, digital sociology is home to a preponderance of individuals in non-research jobs within university administrations, as well as in roles such as librarian, museum curator and the catch-all category of "independent scholar." Indeed, digital sociology emerges during a time when it is increasingly difficult to secure employment as a university academic in any discipline at all. What Weller describes as lower "thresholds to access" therefore means that digital technologies are supporting the intellectual activities of early career, untenured and/or adjunct sociologists, all of whom are pursuing their intellectual passions without the safety net of full-time tenured academic employment. Digital sociology could therefore be seen as an inclusive field of study that operates around (and in between) traditional academic structures and boundaries. This stems directly from the acceptance of digital practices as a primary means of "doing" digital sociology.

The distinct nature of digital sociology practices

Digital sociology is an area driven by distinct ways of engaging with sociological work through digital means. These practices could all be seen to reflect what Weller described earlier as an embrace of networked ways of interacting and are illustrated in four broad areas of activity – i.e. communicating and interacting, writing and publishing, teaching and pedagogy, and engaging with publics beyond academia.

(i) Interactions between digital sociologists

One of the most notable shifts in academic practice over the past twenty years has been the rise of digital communication and interaction between academics around the world. Unsurprisingly, then, digital media is a *de facto* means of how digital sociologists become more knowledgeable, find things out, and communicate information. This is especially the case with social media, where questions are posed, information is passed on, and references and links to work are shared. Social media is also a valuable means of keeping "in the loop" – from announcing calls for papers and funding opportunities through to job offers and irrelevant gossip. In this sense, the idea of "digital sociology" has been formed and sustained largely through social media platforms and practices.

For many digital sociologists, this interactive engagement is most frequently experienced through so-called academic Twitter. While other social media are used by academics, this particular platform has developed into a distinctive space for scholarly interactions. Weller talks in enthusiastic terms of his own personal networks of thousands of different contacts, arguing that Twitter provides him with "an interdisciplinary network" par excellence. Certainly, the notion of digital sociology continues to be explored and expanded through the judicious use of hash-tags such as #DigitalLabor, #Sociology and, of course, #DigitalSociology. The influence of Twitter on academic practice is reflected in the changing nature of the traditionally stuffy and staid academic conference cycle. Now academic conferences are notable for high numbers of people participating remotely, the backchannel of conversation that takes place on platforms such as Twitter, alternative session formats (such as "un-conferences," "teach-meets," and so on), and offline social events where already digitally connected collegial groups gather to meet on a rare face-to-face basis. Small-scale digital sociology conferences and symposia are followed online by many more people than those attending in person, and a few events now take place wholly online.

As might be expected, Twitter is better suited to some forms of academic exchange than others. Academics soon have to get used to operating in a different register – as Stewart (2016) puts it, "navigat[ing] the cognitive dissonance between orality-based expectations of sociality and print-based interpretations of speech." One of the appealing features of a tweet – limited to messages of 280 characters – is the lack of verbose academic discourse and waffle. Twitter is great for "Did you see?" or "Isn't this interesting?" type of interactions, hence the popularity of posts beginning with acronyms such as ICYMI ("in case you missed it"). Twitter also favors bold visualizations and snappy data presentations. Kieran Healy (2017: 778) praises the reach of "a simple graphic summarizing a bus-ride's worth of data analysis." On the other hand, reasoned discussions often tend to progress less successfully. Any interaction that might benefit from elaboration or clarification either migrates quickly to a different medium or else abruptly ceases. As Healy (ibid.: 776) concludes, academic Twitter is marked by "the tendency toward low engagement and rapid bouncing around."

Such uses of digital media therefore make digital sociology practices more immediate but not necessarily more straightforward. Through digital technology, the research community is no longer confined to the institution in which one works and the conferences that one can attend. From a positive point of view, it is argued that the dictum of "publish or perish" might be now reinterpreted as "platform and flourish" (Frost 2017), since some emerging digital sociologists amass considerable online academic reputations well before being awarded a tenured post. Yet digital communication is fraught with issues of public presentation of self. Social media have certainly emerged as an integral element "of constructing and performing the professional self for many workers in higher education" (Lupton 2014: 66). Thus there are obvious rewards and risks associated with being "seen" as a social media academic and the vulnerabilities of sharing one's "private deliberations in a public space" (Rainford 2016: 102).

(ii) Digital sociology writing

Of course, the thoughts of digital sociologists are not expressed exclusively through social media sass and snark – a large part of sociological scholarship remains "academic writing." Here, too, digital technology has impacted significantly on the ways in which sociologists write and how this writing is then seen. Digital sociologists are involved in a variety of different forms of academic writing, all of which are increasingly entwined and iterative in nature. For example, rather than devoting months to crafting a solitary 8,000-word journal article in the hope of its eventually becoming recognized as a magnum opus, many digital sociologists are happy to spend time riffing ideas on Twitter and later rounding these up to a few "blog-worthy" paragraphs. This might then morph into slightly longer and more polished pieces for outlets such as Medium, The Conversation or Huffington Post. Subsequent longer articles might then be directed toward various options – from open-access online titles such as *Sociological Research Online* through to one of the "print" journal titles. In these latter cases, "pre-publication" versions of the article might be posted to paywall-free sites such as Academia.edu, SocArXiv or university open repositories.

These varied forms of output also have a significant influence on the rhythm of academic writing. Many academic authors now engage in what might be termed serial "bricolage," writing in short bursts and garnering public responses to segments of material that might later be reworked and reconstituted in parts of a journal article or even a whole book. Thus, as Deborah Lupton (2014: 79) observes, "there is no longer an end-point to a publication, as its online form can be continually reworked, revised, mashed-up and otherwise transformed continually. This brings up the idea of the circulation of digital material on the internet and how such material may be constantly reinvented." For this reason, in contrast to its declining popularity elsewhere, blogging continues to find favor with academic audiences. Melissa Gregg (2006) praises academic blogging as a valuable form of "conversational scholarship," with many academics welcoming the opportunity for "slow thinking" and the iterative generation of ideas and knowledge sharing (Mewburn and Thomson 2017). Indeed, digital technologies also support collective forms of writing such as the movement of #ShutUpAndWrite groups coordinated through Twitter. There have even been a few instances of crowdsourced co-authoring of whole journal articles through collaborative tools such as Google Docs or Wikispaces (e.g. Al Lily 2016).

Many of the options listed above reflect growing motivations for academics to share access to their written output on a free-of-charge basis. This support for "the academic gift economy" (Lupton 2014: 77) in part reflects a belief in scholarship as a social good, as well as self-interest in getting one's work read as widely as possible. While most academics still shy away from self-publishing, there has been a recent resurgence of academic presses producing books that are distributed online free of charge and sold only in physical form. This has seen calls from some commentators for universities to embrace fully a "pirate philosophy" where academic writing is freely copied and redistributed (Hall 2016).

Of course, despite these good intentions, most digital sociologists still aspire to publish in the high-status outlets operated by commercial academic publishers. Thus the process of writing journal articles, book chapters and academic monographs continues to involve scholars engaging with a digitally driven academic publishing industry that is almost unrecognizable from academic publishing twenty years ago. For example, the dominance of online rather than physical distribution has led to a number of changes in the form and nature of academic publishing. A full-length monograph is now required to be planned and written in an "unbundled" form – i.e. with each chapter appearing in a standalone format with separate abstracts, keywords, and lack of cross-referencing. The old standard monograph of 80,000 words is being replaced by the "rapid" response "pivot" format of 20,000 to 40,000 words. Some texts are sold only in e-book format, with print-on-demand options for the occasional customer wanting a paper version. Similarly, while most of the prestigious academic journals operate behind expensive paywalls priced for institutional "block" subscriptions, an individual article can be designated "open access" at a cost to the author of around $2,000 to $3,000. Article titles, abstracts and keywords are now expected to be crafted with a primary emphasis on "search engine optimization." This means, for example, that article titles are now brief and to the point – with no puns or clever allusions and limited to a length of no more than seventy characters (after which Google will truncate them with ellipses). All told, writing for academic publication is a much altered proposition from what it was even ten years ago.

(iii) Digital sociology pedagogy

Another important aspect of digital sociology is teaching. On the one hand, this relates to opportunities to teach sociology using digital approaches – particularly on a "public pedagogy" basis where education is supported outside of institutionalized educational settings (Giroux 2003). These efforts often seek to make use of technology-based open approaches such as "open education resources" and the much hyped "massive open online courses" of a few years ago. These approaches seek to capitalize on what Weller (2011: 85) terms a "pedagogy of abundance." Weller reasons that digital technology has turned many of the traditional assumptions of teaching on their head – i.e. that teaching talent is scarce, that locating good teaching talent is difficult, that content must be physical, that content is manufactured to demand, and that access to content is scarce (ibid.). Many digital scholars see these developments as supporting the reimagining of education provision in subjects such as sociology. The argument is made that education can be provided in qualitatively and quantitatively different ways, with content and expert knowledge made freely available to be accessed and shared by mass numbers of learners. Teaching is no longer a case of expert-led instruction; rather, it is supporting individuals to learn how to make connections, develop the capacity to know more, nurture and maintain connections to support continual learning, and be able to choose what is best to learn at any particular time.

Second – and perhaps of more significance for digital sociology – are new opportunities to teach about digital topics and issues along sociological lines. As might be expected, digital sociology researchers are also beginning to develop and deliver courses around their topics of expertise. There are burgeoning graduate and post-graduate programs in "digital sociology," "digital society" and "digital media and society." There is also growing interest in developing teaching provision that harnesses the interdisciplinary nature of digital sociology. This relates to the teaching of technology and computational subjects to social science students, as well as the reciprocal teaching of social science subjects to technology and computer-related students. This has seen the growth of courses being taught to sociology majors on topics such as R, Python and "data carpentry." Conversely, there are efforts to teach issues surrounding morals, ethics and society to engineering and computer science students. In addition, there is the development of "critical digital literacy" courses and provision. These are avowedly political reflections on digital technology and society – seeking to support what Emejulu and McGregor (2018) describe as "radical digital citizenship," and focus on critically analyzing the social, political, economic and environmental consequences of technologies in everyday life. Critical digital literacy courses often seek to support students to "collectively deliberate and take action to build alternative and emancipatory technologies and technological practices" (ibid.). In this sense, digital sociology offers an alternative to the apolitical, skills-based teaching of "digital literacy" that has developed in many levels of school and university education.

Third, there are clear implications for the orientation, training and preparation of professional sociologists at all stages of their careers. For example, meaningful engagement with the research methods outlined in chapter 3 requires various practical skills in interrogating software and code and in handling digital data alongside expanding people's "methodological imagination" in terms of the epistemological possibilities of digital techniques and tools (Marres 2017). Similarly, the various facets of "digital scholarship" just outlined in this chapter demand considerable amounts of practice. Of course, much of this knowledge can be developed through sustained personal engagement with the digital. In many instances, the most straightforward way of learning to be a digital sociologist is simply "doing" digital sociology – experimenting with digital tools and techniques and developing through experiential learning. While it is not necessary to reach the status of a fully expert user, it certainly helps if digital sociologists are adept and flexible. There is much to be said for being able quickly to get to grips with the various devices, systems and software that we encounter in our studies.

Yet, while much can be "learned on the job," some aspects of digital sociology undoubtedly require more structured approaches to development. Thus a major challenge is rethinking what "professional development" might now entail for sociologists. Here, a number of leads can be taken from developments in the digital humanities and allied subjects. For example, efforts to develop the technical skills of scholars working in the digital humanities suggest a need to look beyond "Coding 101" courses that provide a knowledge of programming languages and programming concepts. As Peirson et al. (2016) note, while some degree of technical competency is welcome, the ability to engage broadly with technical processes is more desirable than any specific ability to lead or conduct complex technological work.

Thus, instead of being trained to be data scientists or computer programmers per se, sociologists might more usefully be trained as "mediators" between sociological and computational communities. This suggests the development of "hybrid expertise" – i.e. skills and competencies to communicate and cooperate effectively with software engineers. Peirson et al. (2016) suggest that these "soft" skills can be developed by non-expert scholars being embedded within software engineering projects through work-based placements and internships. These secondments can position social scientists as participant observers who engage in "candid interactions" with software engineers and become adept at translating sociological concerns into a computational framework. Such knowledge can also be developed by sociologists being supported to "build their own" software. Regardless of the quality of any final products, the main benefit here is learning about software development processes and cultures. Peirson suggests that involvement in open source communities might be one low-stakes way of participating in software development.

All these latter suggestions involve professional sociologists reaching out to other disciplines. Many of the professional learning activities just described are best conducted in collaboration with computer scientists, data scientists and information specialists – all of whom stand to benefit equally from working alongside sociologists. While digital sociologists have already proven to be remarkably adept at self-organizing such activities along informal lines, clearly universities and faculties can begin to take more responsibility for providing such training. There is also scope for scholarly societies and professional associations to take a broader role in developing the digital capacities of their members. Indeed, the initial growth of digital sociology throughout the 2010s benefited from support from organizations such as the British Sociological Association and the Eastern Sociological Society. While to date it has developed largely *outside* of formal university bureaucracy, if digital sociology is to become an embedded, integral element of the discipline, there is an increasing requirement for institutional support.

iv) Public digital sociology

All these previous examples of digital sociology practice relate mainly to what can be done for groups of academics and students. In contrast, another important strand of digital sociology relates to what is described as "public sociology." Following Michael Burawoy's calls in the 2000s for sociologists to work toward the challenge "to engage multiple publics in multiple ways" (Burawoy 2005: 4), the imperative to engage in public sociology has been widely recognized. While some other areas of sociological inquiry might not have a ready public component, the topics and tools of digital sociology certainly take sociologists well beyond the academy.

In one sense, it is tempting to imagine that any instance of working online is a form of public accessibility and engagement. Healy (2017: 771) describes social media facilitating "a distinctive field of public conversation, exchange, and engagement" between academics and academic publics. Social media certainly make it easier for sociologists "to be seen" and, it follows, make it easier to "see" sociology in action. However, doubts remain over how engaging these public actions actually are. For example, after analyzing 153,000 tweets from 130 sociologists, Schneider and Simonetto (2017: 243) concluded that most were using Twitter primarily to generate information and "publish academic materials in publicly accessible spaces" with little sustained follow-up engagement with publics. Most often, Twitter was being used to "selectively engag[e] with colleagues about research matters" ibid.).

Thus simply working online seems, at best, to meet Burawoy's criteria for "traditional public sociology" – i.e. the online equivalent of writing opinion pieces for print media and offering comments on "matters of public importance." While this work is useful, it hardly fulfills the idea of "organic" public engagement – what Burawoy (2005: 8) describes as sociologists engaging in dialogue with members of the public in "a process of mutual education." In contrast, then, some digital sociologists are also exploring how meaningful forms of public sociology can be supported through more elaborate uses of digital technology.

For example, promising examples of this type of engagement have made use of digital technology to engage large numbers of public collaborators in what might be termed "citizen social science." As with the "citizen science" movement in environmental sciences, these activities support mass participation in research activities, thereby engaging the public in all stages of the research process. Mike Savage's "Great British Class Survey" (Savage et al. 2013) was one such example – using digital tools (notably a web-based "class calculator") and various forms of online dissemination and discussion to engage over 9 million people across the UK to explore the changing dimensions of social class. The project data-sets from the survey sample of 325,000 respondents were made publicly available through the UK Data Service, and public discussions were sustained through activities brokered through the BBC, newspapers and other forums. This is seen as a largely successful attempt to initiate a national conversation about social class underpinned by the use of simple but accessible digital tools.

The Great British Class Survey reflects growing interest in using digital media to make social data available for public analysis and consumption. In the UK, Cardiff University's "COSMOS" platform was developed as a publicly accessible digital observatory, offering various computational tools for harvesting, analyzing and visualizing social media data streams. Yet, such efforts to stimulate online public sociology are not as straightforward as they might appear. While it reached an agreement with Twitter in 2010 to archive every tweet ever posted in the US, the Library of Congress has still to work out how to make this vast, expanding archive accessible to the public, and recently it scaled back its initial ambitions. As Michael Zimmer reflected, "this is a warning as we start dealing with Big Data – we have to be careful what we sign up for" (cited in Daley 2017).

Finally, alongside these consensus-related forms of public engagement are more radical, politically driven approaches toward public sociology based around online forms of activism, advocacy and agitating for rights. For example, research around critical data studies is directed toward enhancing public understandings of data privacy and dataveillance, as well as alternative actions that advantage citizens rather than corporations. These include the co-constructed personal data projects outlined in chapter 4, alongside events such as Alison Powell's "Data Walking" initiative, where researchers lead community explorations of local data industry infrastructure – all efforts to support greater public understanding of contemporary data-intensive digital culture. Kennedy and Moss (2015) describe such activities as working toward the cultivation of "knowing publics" – i.e. publics who are knowledgeable about their engagements with digital technology, therefore increasing the potential for digital societies to know better themselves.

Other forms of public engagement with digital politics include more direct interventions. One high-profile example is the ongoing work of Trebor Scholz, a scholar-activist who has done much to define the field of "digital labor" outlined in chapter 3, while also advocating and agitating toward the establishment of platform cooperativism. This has seen Scholz and his colleagues work with local groups, lawyers and developers in order to establish cooperative platforms around the world to support the ethical "gig" employment of workers. Successful examples range from platforms brokering the services of refugee software programmers in Berlin to house cleaners in New York City. Scholz's form of scholar-activism demonstrates the possibility of working toward the practical addressing of issues raised by academic digital sociology. From this perspective, to paraphrase Karl Marx, the point of digital sociology is not only to interpret the digital world but also to change it.

Critical perspectives on "digital scholarship"

Whether striving to redefine the platform economy or simply share tips on Twitter about how best to teach introductory Durkheim, digital sociologists are clearly working in markedly different ways than might have been the case a few years previously. In fact, it could be argued that contemporary sociologists are compelled to engage in many of these practices. It is increasingly impossible for academics to avoid communicating with other academics online, teaching students online and/or engaging with the digital publishing industry. Whether they are aware of it or not, it could be said that all sociologists now engage in "latently public, ambiently visible" work (Healy 2017: 780).

Yet these new forms of digital sociology practice – and the work that is involved – require close attention (Allmer and Bulut 2018). If digital sociology takes pride in its capacity to remain circumspect about digital promises and technological solutions, then any excitement over the digital scholar needs to be approached with similar scrutiny. While there is much to admire in the enthusiasm of the "digital scholar" turn, it sometimes seems that these messages are tone-deaf to the politics of contemporary academic work. It could be argued that any embrace of digital scholarship ignores the problematic issues of digital labor politics, performativity and affect which need to be thought through more thoroughly (Woodcock 2018). These are all issues that digital sociologists are well used to discussing with regard to other people's digital media use. Amid the general enthusiasm for digital scholarship, there is growing need for some sociological critique and pushback.

First, if we see digital scholarship as a form of digital work, then it takes on a less empowering tone. It is important to acknowledge that digital sociology emerges at a time when academic sociologists are increasingly struggling to engage in sociological research. These are times of reduced funding for social science research, justified on the grounds of austerity and a steady shift away from funding the social sciences and humanities in preference to "proper" science. Put bluntly, sociological research is no longer deemed as fashionable or necessary as it once was. As such, the "agile," "innovative" and "guerrilla" practices outlined above all work in the favor of institutions and governments looking to divest disciplines such as sociology. Innovative practices such as "open access" resources, "crowdfunding" research projects, and so on, can be seen as low-cost alternatives to the proper funding and resourcing of sociology.

Moreover, it is important not to see the activities and practices described earlier as frictionless and effort-free. Many of these practices and approaches constitute additional (and potentially exploitative) work for academics and others around them. For example, maintaining a regular scholarly presence on channels such as Twitter or Academia.edu involves a considerable amount of unpaid academic labor. Similarly, the "rock star" lecturer broadcasting their wisdom to masses of students through a MOOC relies on the support of a range of labor from others behind the scenes. Most forms of online education rely on the casual labor of teaching assistants, e-learning support staff and other low-paid colleagues (Freund et al. 2017). Similarly, freely accessible outlets such as The Conversation and SocArXiv are reliant on considerable behind-the-scenes (often voluntary) labor. None of these innovations happen of their own accord.

Similarly, the capacity of digital sociology to accommodate sociologists working outside of the university system can be seen as problematic. Digital sociology emerges at a time when a majority of people pursing doctorates in academic sociology research will not end up working in full-time academic positions. Most young academics can expect to move job types and sectors during their working lives (Locke et al. 2016). While some are able to make a living as freelancers, increasing numbers of sociology PhDs are compelled to work outside the academy. Again, digital sociology could be seen as an enabler for institutions and funders looking to reduce costs and overheads associated with fully staffed, fully funded academic disciplines. There is a danger that digital sociology becomes the preserve of independently resourced part-time practitioners – a field reliant on people engaging in sociological work in their own (free) time and at their own expense.

Second, then, is the growing co-opting of these forms of digital scholarship into forms of performativity, accountability and measurement-based management that now pervade contemporary academia. This is sometimes presented in empowering terms. For example, it is argued that sociologists have all manner of indicators they can now draw upon in order to gain a sense of their online impact – from the number of followers and likes, through to who is downloading one's writing and from which part of the world. These measures combine to form "the academic quantified self" (Honan et al. 2015: 44). As our previous critiques of digital data suggest, such forms of feedback do not function solely in the interests of individual academics. This is particularly the case with metrics pertaining to reflect the "value" of academic writing and, it is extrapolated, the value of academics as writers. As Roger Burrows (2012) puts it, all academics are now "living with the H-index" – i.e. subject to various forms of "quantified control," accountability and auditing that stem in no small part from many of the digitized writing, publishing and dissemination practices described earlier.

Indeed, a profitable bibliometrics and citations industry has emerged to sell tools and analytics to universities eager to gauge the value of the academics that they employ. This includes various permeations of data related to official citations, which allow authors' success to be calculated in terms of an H-index, i10-index or mquotient. This logic is extended to other possible indicators of impact and engagement. For example, publishers and university authorities are making increasing use of so-called alt-metric measures – pertaining to reflect the social media impact of any article or book. Successful writing is now equated with maximizing one's number of clicks, views, downloads, recommends, shares, tweets and retweets. As Duffy (2017: 1) argues, the influence of "social media logic" is far removed from what academics might consider "the university's knowledge-making ideals."

The heightened accountability of online academic work clearly contributes to the fraught working conditions of contemporary academia. As Healy (2017: 771) reasons, the "attention economy" of academic work online creates "conditions for a new wave of administrative and market elaboration in the field of public conversation ... encourage[ing] new methods of monitoring, and new systems of punishment and reward for participation." The enhanced significance of online attention and "status" could be argued to be commodifying academics' actions in divisive ways. For example, universities now are keen to publicize academics whom they consider to be social media "stars," while at the same time censuring those whose social media activities do not chime with the institutional "brand." Social media are no longer something that an academic engages with on a personal basis.

Indeed, the work of most academics is becoming shaped by these prevailing conditions of metricization and the diminishment of writers to the status of content provider. Some individuals are adept at working in ways that "game" these systems – writing in a manner that mimics the popular online vernacular of clickbait content. Even if they are not engaging in such nefarious practices, the need to write in a manner that results in online impact is influencing what academics do. For example, being restricted to title lengths of seventy characters which feature keywords best suited to Google's search algorithm might seem like a minor inconvenience but marks a significant imposition on the freedom of academics to create knowledge. Crucially, as Burrows (2012: 368) contends, any academic who engages in online publishing and working through social media platforms is therefore "fully implicated" in the enactment of these forms of measurement and metricized scholarship: "we are all involved in the co-construction of statistics and organizational life."

Questions also need to be raised about the affective risks and conflicts inherent in digital scholarship work. Online academic communities reflect the best and worst characteristics of online communities in general. Digital sociologists are not immune to online acts of self-promotion, self-aggrandizement, over-sharing and passive-aggressive interaction. Indeed, it could be argued that digital sociologists can sometimes lapse into behaviors and practices that they might demean in others but of which they are less aware in their own online conduct. In many ways, social media amplify some of the less edifying aspects of academic life. For example, the emergence of online micro-celebrities in digital sociology replicates the hierarchizing of academic disciplines by "big names" and "celebrity dons." Similarly, despite talk of collaboration and interdisciplinary work, academia continues to operate along competitive lines. Grants, paper acceptances and job promotions are all finite resources being competed for by ever-growing numbers of scholars. At best, then, many academics could be said to engage in forms of selective – if not strategic – sharing. One can see how not every sociologist might experience digital scholarship as a completely collegial practice.

Indeed, there are aspects of digital scholarship that might be termed challenging. By working with online publics, sociologists are inviting multiple publics to contest their work. These include interest groups with particular ideological perspectives to promote, as well as trolls and other online abusers. As Lareau and Muñoz (2017: 19) put it diplomatically, sociologists who work online are exposing themselves to "audiences who do not have a neutral, dispassionate approach. And audiences may not always welcome the sociological analysis or research." Jessie Daniels (2017) argues that this is especially the case for sociologists who are female, queer and/or of color. Even if they are not subjected to personal abuse, then there is a strong chance that "these conflicts can create a turbulent environment where sociologists can lose control of their message" (Lareau and Muñoz 2017: 19). The internet is not the most welcoming place for *all* sociologists to present their work.

Finally, concerns can be raised over the potentially exclusionary nature of digital scholarship. As with any area of academia, digital sociology is not a totally "open" space or a wholly level playing field. Despite being well aware of the phenomenon, digital sociologists are not immune to the social media phenomenon of "filter bubbles." Depending on whom one follows, academic Twitter can come across as a supportive community or a self-congratulatory, smug clique. This sense of a homogeneous digital scholarship is certainly evident in the reproduction of academic hierarchies on platforms such as Twitter. While social media have promoted the careers of a few social media-savvy early career researchers, such success stories are not typical. Instead, established professors will often tend to attract more followers (and engage in fewer "follow-backs"), while established institutional "brands" often continue to carry more credibility in the sharing of content (see, for example, Jäschke et al. 2017).

Other forms of digital scholarship are also structured by the "network effects" that are exploited so effectively by companies such as Uber and Amazon. For example, there has been much recent excitement over the possibility of academics raising crowdfunding for their research through platforms such as Experiment.com. Yet the academics who are most successful in raising money in this way are those with expansive social networks, most notably their respective "reach" through online social media (Palmer and Verhoeven 2016). Given the trend for established professorial "names" to attract the largest social media following, there is a danger that trends such as crowdfunding increase the privilege of high-status academics rather than representing an alternative way of working around the system.

Conclusions: so what is digital sociology?

As these latter points illustrate, it is important that sociologists maintain critical distance from their own digital practices and passions. Developments such as "academic Twitter" and online publishing are no less problematic than any other aspect of digital society. Enthusiasms for digital scholarship should be tempered by concerns over unpaid labor, inequalities of participation, discrimination, and the like. Digital sociologists need to be as questioning and skeptical of their own digital practices as they are of the practices of others. Yet, beyond the need to be self-aware and reflexive, what else can be concluded about the question of "What is digital sociology?"? We therefore conclude the book with a set of final reflections on the benefits of taking digital sociology seriously.

The work reviewed over the course of this book certainly offers a critical perspective on what might otherwise appear to be relentless and unfathomable social change. In particular, digital sociology provides rich insights into the ways in which social life increasingly revolves around entanglements of code and physical space, human and non-human actors, and the automated generation and processing of data. While such shifts are being explored across many disciplines, digital sociology seems particularly adept at pointing to associated changes in social relations, social structure and social processes. For example, it is well placed to explore what it means to live in conditions where power and control is exercised though digital profiles, permissions and protocols. Digital sociology helps us understand the growing dominance of reconstituted and intensified forms of technology-based capital accumulation. And it challenges the idea that these changes can be governed only along profit-hungry lines of transnational tech-industry interests.

As has been argued throughout this book, digital sociology is able to make good sense of such shifts through the appropriation of interdisciplinary theory and methods and new modes of scholarly work. Crucially, this involves subjecting "sociology" to a number of necessary relocations. This chapter has considered, for example, how various forms of digital sociology work take place in predominantly online spaces. Elsewhere, we have discussed how digital sociology routinely looks beyond established disciplinary boundaries of "sociology," and often outside the academy altogether. All told, digital sociology is pushing the discipline in a number of new directions and dispositions.

Yet, it would be misleading to reach a set of conclusions about digital sociology that are too neat and tidy. It is important to acknowledge that there is not a unified approach to digital sociology with one consistent narrative. As with all areas of sociology, there will always be disagreement and contention over what digital sociology is and what it is not. People will continue to hold different views of what methods are most insightful and which theories are most perceptive and probing. In this sense, asking ten different authors to write a book such as this would undoubtedly result in ten significantly different lines of argument. Crucially, though, digital sociology thrives on its capacity to accommodate difference. This is an open field rather than a closed shop, and it has already proven a welcoming home for diverse perspectives, interests and convictions about the digital. Most importantly, coming together under the aegis of digital sociology offers a way of bringing these different approaches into dialogue (and hopefully collaboration) with each other.

One important theme that has emerged throughout this book is the ways in which digital sociology is intrinsically rooted in – rather than fundamentally opposed to – a long history of sociological work that precedes it. Digital sociology poses questions about technology that have long been asked within the discipline. Theoretically, then, much digital sociology work is grounded within traditions stemming back through the twentieth century. For example, methodological debates over the value of Big Data in comparison to "small data" and "thick data" could be seen as continuations of long-standing methodological "paradigm wars" and tussles over "mathematical sociology." Even the ostensibly novel aspects of open, networked digital scholarship map onto broader ongoing debates over how social scientists might best work in public and for the public good. In short, digital sociology is part of an ongoing evolution of the discipline – revitalizing classic sociological concerns while introducing novel (or at least substantially altered) points of contention and curiosity.

Hopefully, then, this book dispels any misconception of digital sociology being a new, superior or radically different form of sociology. It does not look to usurp or demean other areas of sociological work but, instead, is a means of augmenting and expanding sociological inquiry. This contrasts with the recent pushback against developments in the digital humanities, where critics have objected to a "destructiveness toward whatever is considered 'non-digital' among digital partisans" (Golumbia 2017). In contrast, digital sociologists have no interest in being disparaging or dismissive of what has come before. To date, there has been little hubris over the perceived merits of digital sociology in comparison to what might be seen as out-of-date, old-fashioned or "dead" forms of sociology. Sociology is not a competition, and digital sociology should not be placed in opposition to any other part of the discipline.

Returning to a theme raised at the beginning of chapter 2, it could be reasoned that describing the work outlined in this book in specific terms of "sociology" is not particularly helpful. Much of this text has considered critical digital research and writing conducted by scholars who might be sociological in their approach but would not limit themselves to being classified as "sociologists." Indeed, much of the best digital sociology work is being conducted at the interfaces of cultural and media studies, communication and information studies, anthropology, urban geography, and similar outposts of the social sciences and humanities. Tellingly, the journals where such ideas are being explored most vigorously are located beyond traditional catalogues of "sociology" literature. For example, *Big Data & Society, Social Media + Society, New Media & Society* and *Information, Communication & Society* feature a range of insightful digital sociological work alongside research and writing that is definitely non-sociological in approach. In this sense, a narrowly bounded idea of sociology fails to capture fully the sociologically complex work that is being conducted on digital issues and topics.

Nevertheless, continuing to stress the idea of a digital *sociology* remains a useful way of foregrounding long-standing sociological concerns in areas where discussions can otherwise slip quickly into the realms of the superficial and "pop." While there is always room for playful, provocative and creatively subversive approaches, digital sociology is also well placed to reflect our current post-Snowden, post-digital times of dissatisfaction and suspicion of the technologies that we have built for ourselves (or, more accurately, that have been built for us). In this sense, then, digital sociology offers a timely corrective to hitherto optimistic and individually focused accounts of digital society. Locating these discussions specifically in terms of sociology reminds us that this is a time for problematizing rather than celebrating digital technology. Whereas the early 2010s might have seemed an appropriate time for playful, cutesy and optimistic scholarship, the years leading up to the 2020s demand more critically aware and antagonistic approaches toward the technologies that are now dominating society. Sociology pushes us to ask questions of what we are *not* happy with (i.e. what we see as inappropriate and/or unacceptable), what we are going to do about it, and what we might want as an alternative.

Of course, developing a clear sense of the question "What is digital sociology?" now leaves us facing the practical task of making things happen. There is a host of hard work implicit in the development of any academic field. This includes the establishment of spaces that can support and sustain dialogue, such as conferences, journals and graduate courses. There is also considerable intellectual work that remains to be done, such as the various forms of theory-building, co-construction of knowledge, and testing of ideas and approaches outlined in this book. All told, there is plenty of work outstanding for digital sociology to be established as a sustained academic presence. In this sense, digital sociology is perhaps most usefully understood as a "moment" rather than a "movement." Digital sociology is not a unified set of principles to be followed dogmatically. Rather, it is a deliberate refocusing of attention, effort and thinking. Twenty years from now there may well not be a digital sociology per se … but it is highly probable that all elements of sociology will be digital. Forward!

References

Abidin, C. (2017) #familygoals: family influencers, calibrated amateurism, and justifying young digital labor, *Social Media + Society* 3(2), https://doi.org/10.1177/2056305117707191.

Agarwal, S., Bennett, W., Johnson, C., and Walker, S. (2014) A model of crowd enabled organization, *International Journal of Communication* 8: 646–72.

Al Lily, A. (2016) A crowd-authoring project on the scholarship of educational technology, *Information Development* 32(5): 1707–17.

Allmer, T., and Bulut, E. (2018) Academic labour, digital media and capitalism, *tripleC* 16(1): 44–8.

Amin, A., and Thrift, N. (2005) What's left? Just the future, *Antipode* 37(2): 220–38.

Andrejevic, M. (2007) *iSpy: Surveillance and Power in the Interactive Era*. Lawrence: University Press of Kansas.

Aroles, J. (2014) Book review: Trebor Scholtz (ed.), *Digital Labor: The Internet as Playground and Factory*, *Work, Employment and Society* 28(1): 144–5.

Back, L. (2012) Live sociology: social research and its futures, *Sociological Review* 60(S1): 18–39.

Bail, C. (2014) The cultural environment: measuring culture with Big Data, *Theory and Society* 43(3/4): 465–82.

Banks, J., and Deuze, M. (2009) Co-creative labour, *International Journal of Cultural Studies* 12(5): 419–31.

Barratt, M., and Maddox, A. (2016) Active engagement with stigmatised communities through digital ethnography, *Qualitative Research* 16(6): 701–19.

Bauman, Z. (2014) *What Use is Sociology?* Cambridge: Polity [interviews with M. Jacobsen and K. Tester].

Bayne, S. (2015) Teacherbot: interventions in automated teaching, *Teaching in Higher Education* 20(4): 455–67.

Beer, D. (2014) *Punk Sociology*. Basingstoke: Palgrave Macmillan.

Beer, D., and Burrows, R. (2013) Popular culture, digital archives and the new social life of data, *Theory, Culture and Society* 30(4): 47–71.

Belk, R. (2013) Extended self in a digital world, *Journal of Consumer Research* 40(3): 477–500.

Bell, D. ([1973] 1999) *The Coming of Post-Industrial Society*. New York: Basic Books.

Berry, D., and Dieter, M. (2015) *Postdigital Aesthetics: Art, Computation and Design*. Basingstoke: Palgrave Macmillan.

Birkbak, A., and Carlsen, H. (2016) The public and its algorithms: comparing and experimenting with calculated publics, in Amoore, L., and Piotukh, V. (eds), *Algorithmic Life*. Abingdon: Routledge (pp. 21–34).

Bock, M., and Figueroa, E. (2018) Faith and reason: an analysis of the homologies of Black and Blue Lives Facebook pages, *New Media & Society*, https://doi.org/10.1177/1461444817740822.

Bodle, R. (2016) A critical theory of advertising as surveillance, in Hamilton, J., Bodle, R., and Korin, E. (eds), *Explorations in Critical Studies of Advertising*. Abingdon: Routledge (pp. 138–52).

Boellstorff, T. (2008) *Coming of Age in Second Life*. Princeton, NJ: Princeton University Press.

Boyd, D., and Crawford, K. (2012) Critical questions for Big Data, *Information, Communication & Society* 15(5): 662–79.

Bratton, B. (2016) *The Stack*. Cambridge, MA: MIT Press.

Brock, A. (2012) From the blackhand side: Twitter as a cultural conversation, *Journal of Broadcasting and Electronic Media* 56(4): 529–49.

Brooker, P., Dutton, W., and Greiffenhagen, C. (2017) What would Wittgenstein say about social media? *Qualitative Research* 17(6): 610–26.

Browne, S. (2010) Digital epidermalization: race, identity and biometrics, *Critical Sociology* 36(1): 131–50.

Bruns, A. (2017) Australian Twitter is more diverse than you think, *The Conversation*, May 3, http://theconversation.com/australian-twitter-is-more-diverse-than-you-think-76864.

Bruns, A., and Hanusch, F. (2017) Conflict imagery in a connective environment, *Media, Culture and Society* 39(8): 1122–41.

Bruns, A., Highfield, T., and Burgess, J. (2013) The Arab Spring and social media audiences, *American Behavioral Scientist* 57(7): 871–98.

Bucher, E., and Fieseler, C. (2017) The flow of digital labor, *New Media & Society* 19(11): 1868–86.

Bunce, M. (2018) Management and resistance in the digital newsroom, *Journalism*, https://doi.org/10.1177/1464884916688963.

Burawoy, M. (2005) For public sociology: 2004 presidential address, *American Sociological Review* 70(1): 4–28.

Burrows, R. (2012) Living with the h-index? Metric assemblages in the contemporary academy, *Sociological Review* 60(2): 355–72.

Burrows, R., and Savage, M. (2014) After the crisis? Big data and the methodological challenges of empirical sociology, *Big Data & Society* 1(1), https://doi.org/10.1177/2053951714540280.

Cansoy, M., and Schor, J. (2016) Who gets to share in the "sharing economy": understanding the patterns of participation and exchange in Airbnb, Unpubd paper, Boston College, www.bc.edu/content/dam/files/schools/cas_sites/sociology/pdf/SharingEconomy.pdf.

Cardullo, P. (2017) Gentrification in the mesh? An ethnography of Open Wireless Network (OWN) in Deptford, *City* 21(3–4): 405–19.

Carrigan, M. (2015) Towards a meta-critique of data science, October 13, https://markcarrigan.net/2015/10/13/towards-a-meta-critique-of-data-science/.

Casilli, A. (2017) Venture labor: how venture labor sheds light on the digital platform economy, *International Journal of Communication* 11(4): 2067–70.

Castells, M. (1996–8) *The Information Age: Economy, Society and Culture*, Vol. 1: *The Rise of the Network Society*; Vol. 2: *The Power of Identity*; Vol. 3: *End of Millennium*. Oxford: Blackwell.

Castells, M. (2000) Materials for an exploratory theory of the network society, *British Journal of Sociology* 51(1): 5–24.

Cavanagh, A. (2013) Imagining networks: the sociology of connection in the digital age, in Orton-Johnson, K., and Prior. N. (eds), *Digital Sociology*. Basingstoke: Palgrave Macmillan (pp. 169–85).

Cheney-Lippold, J. (2017) *We Are Data: Algorithms and the Making of our Digital Selves*. New York: New York University Press.

Christakis, N. (2012) A new kind of social science for the 21st century, *The Edge*, August 21, www.edge.org/conversation/nicholas_a_christakis-a-new-kind-of-social-science-for-the-21st-century.

Chun, W. (2015) Networks NOW: belated too early, in Berry, D., and Dieter, M. (eds), *Postdigital Aesthetics: Art, Computation and Design*. Basingstoke: Palgrave Macmillan (pp. 289–315).

Chun, W. (2016) Updating to Remain the Same: *Habitual New Media*. Cambridge, MA: MIT Press.

Chun, W. (2018) Faculty profile, Brown University, https://vivo.brown.edu/display/wchun.

Clough, P. (2018) *The User Unconscious: On Affect, Media, and Measure*. Minneapolis: Minnesota University Press.

Clough, P., Gregory, K., Haber, B., and Scannell, J. (2015) The datalogical turn, in Vannini, P. (ed.), *Non-Representational Methodologies*. Abingdon: Routledge (pp. 146–64).

Cockburn, C. (1992) The circuit of technology: gender, identity and power, in Hirsch, E., and Silverstone, R. (eds), *Consuming Technologies: Media and Information in Domestic Spaces*. London: Routledge (pp. 32–42).

Cohen, N. (2015a) From pink slips to pink slime: transforming media labor in a digital age, *Communication Review* 18(2): 98–122.

Cohen, N. (2015b) Cultural work as a site of struggle: freelancers and exploitation, in Fuchs, C., and Mosco, V. (eds), *Marx and the Political Economy of the Media*. Boston: Brill (pp. 36–64).

Coté, M., and Pybus, J. (2011) Learning to immaterial labor 2.0: Facebook and social networks, in Peters, M., and Bulut, E. (eds), *Cognitive Capitalism, Education and Digital Labour*. New York: Peter Lang (pp. 169–94).

Coté, M., Gerbaudo, P., and Pybus, J. (2016) Introduction: politics of Big Data, *Digital Culture and Society* 2(2): 5–16.

Cottom, T. (2016) Black cyberfeminism: ways forward for classification situations, intersectionality and digital sociology, in Daniels, J., Cottom, T., and Gregory, K. (eds), *Digital Sociologies*. Bristol: Policy Press (pp. 211–30).

Couldry, N., and Hepp, A. (2016) *The Mediated Construction of Reality*. Cambridge: Polity.

Daley, J. (2017) The Library of Congress will stop archiving Twitter, December 27, www.smithsonianmag.com/smart-news/library-congress-will-stop-archiving-twitter-180967651/#1xrrFrfTYRcsX hfa.99.

Daniels, J. (2009) Cloaked websites: propaganda, cyber-racism and epistemology in the digital era, *New Media & Society* 11(5): 659–83.

Daniels, J. (2013) Race and racism in Internet studies: a review and critique, *New Media & Society* 15(5): 695–719.

Daniels, J. (2015) "My brain database doesn't see skin color": colorblind racism in the technology industry and in theorizing the Web, *American Behavioral Scientist* 59(11): 1377–93.

Daniels, J. (2016) Bodies in code, in Daniels, J., Cottom, T., and Gregory, K. (eds), *Digital Sociologies*. Bristol: Policy Press (pp. 335–8).

Daniels, J. (2017) Interview with Inger Mewburn, in Lupton, D., Mewburn, I., and Thomson P. (eds), *The Digital Academic: Critical Perspectives on Digital Technologies in Higher Education*. Abingdon: Routledge (pp. 162–7).

Daoud, A., and Kohl, S. (2016) *How Much Do Sociologists Write about Economic Topics? Using Big Data to Test Some Conventional Views in Economic Sociology*, 1890 to 2014, Discussion Paper 16/7. Cologne: Max Planck Institut für Gesellschaftsforschung.

De Kosnik, A. (2013) Fandom as free labor, in Scholz, T. (ed.), *Digital Labor: The Internet as Playground and Factory*. New York: Routledge (pp. 98–111).

Dean, J. (2005) Communicative capitalism: circulation and the foreclosure of politics, *Cultural Politics* 1(1): 51–74.

Deleuze, G. (1992) Postscript on the societies of control, *October 59*: 3–7.

Dencik, L. (2017) Paper given at the ECREA Symposium, "Digital Democracy: Critical Perspectives in the Age of Big Data," Stockholm, November 10–11.

DiMaggio, P., Nag, M., and Blei, D. (2013) Exploiting affinities between topic modelling and the sociological perspective on culture, *Poetics* 41(6): 570–606.

Dodds, P., Harris, K., Kloumann, I., Bliss, C., and Danforth, C. (2011) Temporal patterns of happiness and information in a global social network: hedonometrics and Twitter, *PloS one* 6(12): e26752.

Duffy, B. (2017) *(Not) Getting Paid to Do What You Love: Gender, Social Media, and Aspirational Work*. New Haven, CT: Yale University Press.

Duffy, B., and Wissinger, E. (2017) Mythologies of creative work in the social media age: fun, free, and "just being me," *International Journal of Communication* 11: 4652–71.

Dujarier, M. (2015) The activity of the consumer: strengthening, transforming, or contesting capitalism?, *Sociological Quarterly* 56(3): 460–71.

Dutton, W. (2013) Internet studies: the foundations of a transformative field, in Dutton, W. (ed.), *Oxford Handbook of Internet Studies*. Oxford: Oxford University Press (pp. 1–23).

Edelman, B., and Luca, M. (2014) *Digital Discrimination: The Case of Airbnb*, Working Paper 14-054, Harvard Business School, www.hbs.edu/faculty/Publication Files/Airbnb_92dd6086-6e46-4eaf-9cea-60fe5ba3c596.pdf.

Edelman, B., Luca, M., and Svirsky, D. (2016) Racial Discrimination in the Sharing Economy: Evidence from a Field Experiment, Working Paper 16-069, Harvard Business School, www.hbs.edu/faculty/Publication Files/16-069_5c3b2b36-d9f8-4b38-9639-2175aaf9ebc9.pdf.

Ellul, J. (1964) *The Technological Society*. New York: Knopf.

Ellul, J. (1990) *The Technological Bluff* (trans. Bromley, G.). Grand Rapids, MI: Eerdmans.

Elmer, G. (2003) A diagram of panoptic surveillance, *New Media & Society* 5(2): 231–47.

Emejulu, A., and McGregor, C. (2018) Towards a radical digital citizenship in digital education, *Critical Studies in Education*, https://doi.org/10.1080/17508487.2016.1234494.

Evans, L., and Rees, S. (2012) An interpretation of digital humanities, in Berry, D. (ed.), *Understanding Digital Humanities*. Basingstoke: Palgrave Macmillan (pp. 21–41).

Feenberg, A. (1995) *Alternative Modernity: The Technical Turn in Philosophy and Social Theory*. Berkeley: University of California Press.

Fish, A., and Srinivasan, R. (2012) Digital labor is the new killer app, *New Media & Society* 14(1): 137–52.

Fish, A., Garrett, B., and Case, O. (2017) Drones caught in the net, *Imaginations: Journal of Cross-Cultural Image Studies* 8(2), http://imaginations.glendon.yorku.ca/?p=9964.

Flaxman, S., Goel, S., and Rao, J. (2016) Filter bubbles, echo chambers, and online news consumption, *Public Opinion Quarterly* 80(1): 298–320.

Flecker, J., Fibich, T., and Kraemer, K. (2017) Socio-economic changes and the reorganization of work, in Korunka, C., and Kubicek, B. (eds), *Job Demands in a Changing World of Work*. Rotterdam: Springer (pp. 7–24).

Flores-Yeffal, N., Vidales, G., and Martinez, G. (2018). #WakeUp America, #IllegalsAreCriminals: the role of the cyber public sphere in the perpetuation of the Latino cyber-moral panic in the US, *Information, Communication & Society*, https://doi.org/10.1080/1369118X.2017.1388428.

Flores-Yeffal, N., Vidales, G., and Plemons, A. (2011) The Latino cyber-moral panic process in the United States, *Information, Communication & Society* 14(4): 568–89.

Floridi, L. (2014) *The Fourth Revolution: How the Infosphere is Reshaping Human Reality*. Oxford: Oxford University Press.

Freund, K., Kizimchuk, S., Zapasnik, J., Esteves, K., and Mewburn, I. (2017) A labour of love: a critical examination of the "labour icebergs" of massive open online courses, in Lupton, D., Mewburn, I. and Thomson P. (eds), *The Digital Academic: Critical Perspectives on Digital Technologies in Higher Education*. Abingdon: Routledge (pp. 122–39).

Frost, C. (2017) Going from PhD to platform, in Lupton, D., Mewburn, I., and Thomson, P. (eds), *The Digital Academic: Critical Perspectives on Digital Technologies in Higher Education*. Abingdon: Routledge (pp. 36–46).

Fuchs, C., and Dyer-Witheford, N. (2013) Karl Marx @ internet studies, *New Media & Society* 15(5): 782–96.

Fuchs, C., and Sevignani, S. (2013) What is digital labour? What is digital work? What's their difference? And why do these questions matter for understanding social media? *tripleC* 11(2): 237–93.

Fuller, M. (2008) *Software Studies: A Lexicon*. Cambridge, MA: MIT Press.

Galič, M., Timan, T., and Koops, B. (2017) Bentham, Deleuze and beyond: an overview of surveillance theories from the Panopticon to participation, *Philosophy of Technology* 30: 9–37.

Galloway, A., and Thacker, E. (2007) *The Exploit: A Theory of Networks*. Minneapolis: University of Minnesota Press.

Galperin, H., and Greppi, C. (2017) *Geographical Discrimination in the Gig Economy*, Social Science Research Network, https://ssrn.com/abstract=2922874.

Gandy, O. (1993) *The Panoptic Sort*. Boulder, CO: Westview Press.

Garrison, K. (2010) Perpetuating the technological ideology, *Bulletin of Science, Technology and Society* 30(3): 195–204.

Gehl, R. (2016) Power/freedom on the dark web: a digital ethnography of the Dark Web Social Network, *New Media & Society* 18(7): 1219–35.

Geiger, R., and Ribes, D. (2011) Trace ethnography, in *Proceedings of the 44th Annual Hawai'i International Conference on System Sciences*. Los Alamitos, CA: IEEE (pp. 1–10).

Gillborn, D., Warmington, P., and Demack, S. (2018) QuantCrit: education, policy, "Big Data" and principles for a critical race theory of statistics, *Race Ethnicity and Education* 21(2): 158–79.

Gillespie, T. (2016) Algorithm, in Peters, B. (ed.), *Digital Keywords: A Vocabulary of Information Society and Culture*. Princeton, NJ: Princeton University Press (pp. 18–30).

Giroux, H. (2003) Public pedagogy and the politics of resistance: notes on a critical theory of educational struggle, *Educational Philosophy and Theory* 35(1): 5–16.

Golumbia, D. (2017) *The Destructiveness of the Digital Humanities*, June 5, www.uncomputing.org/?p=1868.

Graham, M., Hjorth, I., and Lehdonvirta, V. (2017) Digital labour and development: impacts of global digital labour platforms and the gig economy on worker livelihoods, *Transfer: European Review of Labour and Research* 23(2): 135–62.

Graham, R., and Smith, S. (2016) The content of our #characters: Black Twitter as counterpublic, *Sociology of Race and Ethnicity* 2(4): 433–49.

Graham, T., and Sauter, T. (2013) Google Glass as a technique of self and the revitalisation of the monad, in Osbaldiston, N., Strong, C., and Forbes-Mewett, H. (eds), *TASA 2013: Reflections, Intersections and Aspirations: Proceedings of the Australian Sociological Association 2013 Conference*, Caulfield, VIC, 25–8 November (pp. 1–13).

Gray, K. (2016) "They're just too urban": black gamers streaming on Twitch, in Daniels, J., Cottom, T., and Gregory, K. (eds), *Digital Sociologies*. Bristol: Policy Press (pp. 355–68).

Greaves, M. (2015) The rethinking of technology in class struggle: communicative affirmation and foreclosure politics, *Rethinking Marxism* 27(2): 195–211.

Greenfield, A. (2017) *Radical Technologies*. London: Verso.

Gregg, M. (2006) Feeling ordinary: blogging as conversational scholarship, *Continuum* 20(2): 147–60.

Gregg, M., and Nafus, D. (2017) Data, in Ouellette, L., and Gray, J. (eds), *Keywords for Media Studies*. New York: New York University Press (pp. 55–8).

Gunderson, R. (2016) The sociology of technology before the turn to technology, *Technology in Society* 47: 40–8.

Gupta, N., Crabtree, A., Rodden, T., Martin, D., and O'Neill, J. (2014) Understanding Indian crowdworkers, in *Proceedings of the 17th Conference on Computer Supported Cooperative Work*. New York: ACM (pp. 1–5).

Haber, B. (2016) The queer ontology of digital method, *Women's Studies Quarterly* 44(3/4): 150–69.

Haggerty, K., and Ericson, R. (2000) The surveillant assemblage, *British Journal of Sociology* 51(4): 605–22.

Halford, S., and Savage, M. (2017) Speaking sociologically with Big Data: symphonic social science and the future for Big Data research, *Sociology* 51(6): 1132–48.

Halford, S., Pope, C., and Weal, M. (2013) Digital futures? Sociological challenges and opportunities in the emergent semantic web, *Sociology* 47(1): 173–89.

Hall, G. (2016) *Pirate Philosophy*. Cambridge, MA: MIT Press.

Hannigan, T. (2015) Close encounters of the conceptual kind: disambiguating social structure from text, *Big Data & Society* 2(2), https://doi.org/10.1177/2053951715608655.

Haraway, D. (1985) *A Manifesto for Cyborgs: Science, Technology, and Socialist Feminism in the 1980s*. San Francisco: Center for Social Research and Education.

Hardaker, C., and McGlashan, M. (2016) Real men don't hate women: Twitter rape threats and group identity, *Journal of Pragmatics* 91: 80–93.

Hardt, M., and Negri, A. (2001) *Empire*. Cambridge, MA: Harvard University Press.

Harlow, S., and Benbrook, A. (2018) How #Blacklivesmatter: exploring the role of hip-hop celebrities in constructing racial identity on Black Twitter, *Information, Communication & Society*, https://doi.org/10.1080/1369118X.2017.1386705.

Healy, K. (2017) Public sociology in the age of social media, *Perspectives on Politics* 15: 771–80.

Hine, C. (2015) *Ethnography for the Internet*. London: Bloomsbury.

Hollander, J., and Hartt, M. (2017) Big data and shrinking cities, in Schintler, L., and Chen, Z. (eds), *Big Data for Regional Science*. Abingdon: Routledge (pp. 265–74).

Honan, E., Henderson, L., and Loch, S. (2015) Producing moments of pleasure within the confines of an academic quantified self, *Creative Approaches to Research* 8(3): 44–62.

Hoofd, M. (2014) The London riots and the simulation of sociality in social media research, *Journal of Critical Globalisation Studies* 7: 122–42.

Hope, A. (2016) Biopower and school surveillance technologies 2.0, *British Journal of Sociology of Education* 37(7): 885–904.

Houghton, J., Siegel, M., Madnick, S., Tounaka, N., Nakamura, K., Sugiyama, T., and Shirnen, B. (2018) Beyond keywords: tracking the evolution of conversational clusters in social media, *Sociological Methods & Research* [forthcoming].

Housley, W., Procter, R., Edwards, A., Burnap, P., Williams, M., Sloan, L., Farooq, O., Voss, A., and Greenhill, A. (2014) Big and broad social data and the sociological imagination, *Big Data & Society* 1(2), https://doi.org/10.1177/2053951714545135.

Hughes, K. (2014) "Work/place" media: locating laboring audiences, *Media, Culture and Society* 36(5): 644–60.

Hughes, T. (1983) *Networks of Power: Electrification in Western Society, 1880–1930*. Baltimore: Johns Hopkins University Press.

Ignatow, G., and Robinson, L. (2017) Pierre Bourdieu: theorizing the digital, *Information, Communication & Society* 20(7): 950–66.

Introna, L., and Nissenbaum, H. (2000) Shaping the web: why the politics of search engines matters, *Information Society* 16(3): 169–85.

Irani, L. (2013) The cultural work of microwork infrastructures: hacking Amazon Mechanical Turk, *Selected Papers of Internet Research 14.0*. Denver Association of Internet Researchers, https://spir.aoir.org/index.php/spir/article/viewFile/870/447.

Irani, L. (2017) Mechanical Turk, *Blackwell Encyclopedia of Sociology*. 2nd edn, New York: Wiley-Blackwell (pp. 1–3).

ITU (2017) *Measuring the Information Society Report*. Geneva: International Telecommunication Union.

Jackson, K. (2011) The drive-in culture of contemporary America, in LeGates, R., and Stout, F. (eds), *The City Reader*. 5th edn, London: Routledge (pp. 65–74).

Jameson, F. (1991) *Postmodernism, or, The Cultural Logic of Late Capitalism*. Durham, NC: Duke University Press.

Jarrett, K. (2015) *Feminism, Labour and Digital Media*. Abingdon: Routledge.

Jäschke, R., Linek, S., and Hoffmann, C. (2017) New media, familiar dynamics: academic hierarchies influence academics' following behaviour on Twitter, *LSE Impact Blog*, October 3, http://blogs.lse.ac.uk/impactofsocialsciences/2017/10/03/new-media-familiar-dynamics-academic-hierarchies-influence-academics-following-behaviour-on-twitter/.

Jurgenson, N. (2012) When atoms meet bits: social media, the mobile web and augmented revolution, *Future Internet* 4(1): 83–91, doi:10.3390/fi4010083.

Kennedy, H. (2017) Book review: Noortje Marres, *Digital Sociology: The Re-Invention of Social Research*, *Sociology*, https://doi.org/10.1177/0038038517732257.

Kennedy, H., and Moss, G. (2015) Known or knowing publics? *Big Data & Society* 2(2), https://doi.org/10.1177/2053951715611145.

Kitchin, R., and Dodge, M. (2011) *Code/Space: Software and Everyday Life*. Cambridge, MA: MIT Press.

Kolko, B. (2000) Erasing @race: going white in the (inter)face, in Kolko, B., Nakamura, L., and Rodman, G. (eds), *Race in Cyberspace*. New York: Routledge (pp. 213–32).

Koloğlugil, S. (2015) Digitizing Karl Marx: the new political economy of general intellect and immaterial labor, *Rethinking Marxism* 27(1): 123–37.

Kowalski, R. (1979) Algorithm = logic + control, *Communications of the ACM* 22(7): 424–36.

Kramer, A., Guillory, J., and Hancock, J. (2014) Experimental evidence of massive-scale emotional contagion through social networks, *Proceedings of the National Academy of Sciences* 111(24): 8788–90.

Kuehn, K., and Corrigan, T. (2013) Hope labor: the role of employment prospects in online social production, *Political Economy of Communication* 1(1), www.polecom.org/index.php/polecom/article/view/9/64.

Lane, L. (2016) The digital street: an ethnographic study of networked street life in Harlem, *American Behavioral Scientist* 60(1): 43–58.

Langlois, G., and Elmer, G. (2013) The research politics of social media platforms, *Culture Machine* 14: 1–17.

Lareau, A., and Muñoz, V. (2017) Conflict in public sociology, *Sociological Quarterly* 58(1): 19–23.

Latour, B. (1987) *Science in Action*. Cambridge, MA: Harvard University Press.

Lazer, D., Pentland, A., Adamic, L., Aral, S., Barabasi, A., Brewer, D., and Jebara, T. (2009) Life in the network: the coming age of computational social science, *Science* 323(5915): 721–3.

Lee-Won, R., White, T., and Potocki, B. (2018) The black catalyst to tweet, *Information, Communication & Society* 21(8): 1097–115.

Leurs, K., and Shepherd, T. (2017) Datafication and discrimination, in Schäfer, M., and van Es, K. (eds), *The Datafied Society: Studying Culture through Data*. Amsterdam: Amsterdam University Press (pp. 211–34).

Levina, M. (2017) Network, in Ouellette, L., and Gray, J. (eds), *Keywords for Media Studies*. New York: New York University Press (pp. 127–9).

Lindgren, S. (2017) *Digital Media and Society*. London: Sage.

Locke, W., Whitchurch, C., Smith, H., and Mazenod, A. (2016) *Shifting Landscapes: Meeting the Staff Development Needs of the Changing Academic Workforce*. York: Higher Education Academy.

Lovink, G. (2011) *Networks without a Cause: A Critique of Social Media*. Cambridge: Polity.

Lupton, D. (2014) *Digital Sociology*. Abingdon: Routledge.

Lupton, D. (2016) The diverse domains of quantified selves: self-tracking modes and dataveillance, *Economy and Society* 45(1): 101–22.

Lupton, D., Mewburn, I., and Thomson P. (2017) The digital academic: identities, contexts and politics, in Lupton, D., Mewburn, I., and Thomson P. (eds), *The Digital Academic: Critical Perspectives* on *Digital Technologies in Higher Education*. Abingdon: Routledge (pp. 1–19).

Lyon, D. (2014) Surveillance, Snowden, and Big Data: capacities, consequences, critique, *Big Data & Society* 1(2), https://doi.org/10.1177/2053951714541861.

Mackenzie, A. (2017) *Machine Learners: Archaeology of a Data Practice*. Cambridge, MA: MIT Press.

Maddox, A. (2016) Beyond digital dualism, in Daniels, J., Cottom, T., and Gregory, K. (eds), *Digital Sociologies*. Bristol: Policy Press (pp. 9–26).

Maley, T. (2004) Max Weber and the iron cage of technology, *Bulletin of Science, Technology and Society* 24(1): 69–86.

Malin, B., and Chandler, C. (2017) Free to work anxiously: splintering precarity among drivers for Uber and Lyft, *Communication, Culture and Critique* 10(2): 382–400.

Mann, R. (2012) Five minutes with Prabhakar Raghavan: Big Data and social science at Google, *Impact of Social Sciences*, http://blogs.lse.ac.uk/impactofsocialsciences/2012/09/19/five-minutes-with-prabhakar-raghavan.

Marcuse, H. ([1964] 1991) *One-Dimensional Man*. 2nd edn, London: Routledge.

Marres, N. (2017) *Digital Sociology: The Reinvention of Social Research*. Cambridge: Polity.

Matamoros-Fernández, A. (2017) Platformed racism: the mediation and circulation of an Australian race-based controversy on Twitter, Facebook and YouTube, *Information, Communication & Society* 20(6): 930–46.

Mattern, S. (2016) Interfacing urban intelligence, in Kitchin, R., and Perng, S. (eds), *Code and the City*. New York: Routledge (pp. 49–60).

Matthewman, S. (2011) *Technology and Social Theory*. Basingstoke: Palgrave Macmillan.

McFall, E., and Deville, J. (2017) The market will have you, in Cochoy, F., Deville, J., and McFall, E. (eds), *Markets and the Arts of Attachment*. Abingdon: Routledge (pp. 108–31).

McFarland, D., Lewis, K., and Goldberg, A. (2016) Sociology in the era of Big Data: the ascent of forensic social science, *American Sociologist* 47(1): 12–35.

Mewburn, I., and Thomson, P. (2017) Towards an academic self: blogging during the doctorate, in Lupton, D., Mewburn, I., and Thomson P. (eds), *The Digital Academic: Critical Perspectives on Digital Technologies in Higher Education*. Abingdon: Routledge (pp. 20–35).

Michael, M. (2012) De-signing the object of sociology: toward an 'idiotic' methodology, *Sociological Review* 60(1): 166–83.

Morozov, E. (2011) e-Salvation, *The New Republic*, March 3, https://newrepublic.com/article/84525/morozov-kelly-technology-book-wired.

Mumford, L. ([1934] 2010) *Technics and Civilization.* Chicago: University of Chicago Press.

Mumford, L. (1970) *The Pentagon of Power.* San Diego: Harcourt Brace Jovanovich.

Murthy, D., Powell, A., Tinati, R., Anstead, N., Carr, L., Halford, S., and Weal, M. (2016) Bots and political influence: a sociotechnical investigation of social network capital, *International Journal of Communication* 10: 4952–71.

Mützel, S. (2015) Facing Big Data: making sociology relevant, *Big Data & Society* 1(1), https://doi.org/10.1177/2053951715599179.

Nakamura, L., and Chow-White, P. (2013) *Race after the Internet.* Abingdon: Routledge.

Nakayama, T. (2017) What's next for whiteness and the internet? *Critical Studies in Media Communication* 34(1): 68–72.

Neate, R. (2018) Apple leads race to become world's first $1tn company, *The Guardian*, January 3, www.theguardian.com/business/2018/jan/03/apple-leads-race-to-become-world-first-1tn-dollar-company.

Niesen, M. (2016) Love Inc., in Noble, S., and Tynes, B. (eds), *The Intersectional Internet.* New York: Peter Lang (pp. 161–78).

Noble, S. (2018) *Algorithms of Oppression.* New York: New York University Press.

Norris, P. (2001) *Digital Divide: Civic Engagement, Information Poverty, and the Internet Worldwide.* Cambridge: Cambridge University Press.

Ogburn, W. (1936) Technology and governmental change, *Journal of Business of the University of Chicago* 9(1): 1–13.

Ogburn, W., and Thomas, D. (1937) Are inventions inevitable? *Political Science Quarterly* 37(1): 83–98.

Orton-Johnson, K., and Prior, N. (2013) *Digital Sociology: Critical Perspectives.* Basingstoke: Palgrave Macmillan.

Palmer, S., and Verhoeven, D. (2016) Crowdfunding academic researchers: the importance of academic social media profiles, in *ECSM 2016: Proceedings of the 3rd European Conference on Social Media.* Sonning Common, Oxon.: Academic Conferences and Publishing International (pp. 291–9), http://dro.deakin.edu.au/eserv/DU:30084895/palmer-crowdfunding-2016.pdf.

Parisi, L. (2013) *Contagious Architecture: Computation, Aesthetics, and Space.* Cambridge, MA: MIT Press.

Pasquale, F. (2015) The algorithmic self, *Hedgehog Review* 17(1), www.iasc-culture.org/THR/THR_article_2015_Spring_Pasquale.php.

Peirson, B., Damerow, J., and Laubichler, M. (2016) Software development and trans-disciplinary training at the interface of digital humanities and computer science, *Digital Studies/Le champ numérique*, www.digitalstudies.org//article/10.16995/dscn.17/.

Peters, B. (2016) *Digital Keywords: A Vocabulary of Information Society and Culture.* Princeton, NJ: Princeton University Press.

Petitfils, B. (2014) Researching the posthuman paradigm, in Snaza, N., and Weaver, J. (eds), *Posthumanism and Educational Research*. Abingdon: Routledge (pp. 30–42).

Petre, C. (2015) *The Traffic Factories: Metrics at Chartbeat, Gawker Media, and the New York Times*. New York: Tow Center for Digital Journalism.

Pinch, T. (1998) Theoretical approaches to science, technology and social change: recent developments, *Southeast Asian Journal of Social Science* 26(1): 7–16.

Pink, S., Horst, H., Postill, J., Hjorth, L., Lewis, T., and Tacchi, J. (2016) *Digital Ethnography: Principles and Practice*. London: Sage.

Plant, S. (1996) *Zeroes + Ones: Digital Women and the New Technoculture*. New York: Doubleday.

Poster, M. (1990) *The Mode of Information: Poststructuralism and Social Context*. Chicago: University of Chicago Press.

Pybus, J., Coté, M., and Blanke, T. (2015) Hacking the social life of Big Data, *Big Data & Society* 1(1), https://doi.org/10.1177/2053951715616649.

Quill, L. (2016) Technological conspiracies: Comte, technology, and spiritual despotism, *Critical Review* 28(1): 89–111.

Rainford, J. (2016) Becoming a doctoral researcher in a digital world: reflections on the role of Twitter for reflexivity and the internal conversation, *E-Learning and Digital Media* 13(1–2): 99–105.

Rambukkana, N. (2015) *Hashtag Publics: The Power and Politics of Discursive Networks*. New York: Peter Lang.

Rheingold, H. (2000) *The Virtual Community: Homesteading on the Electronic Frontier*. Cambridge, MA: MIT Press.

Rieder, B., and Röhle, T. (2012) Digital methods: five challenges, in Berry, D. (ed.), *Understanding Digital Humanities*. Basingstoke: Palgrave Macmillan (pp. 67–84).

Ritzer, G. (1993) *The McDonaldization of Society: An Investigation into the Changing Character of Contemporary Social Life*. Newbury Park, CA: Pine Forge Press.

Ritzer, G. (2013) The technological society: social theory, McDonaldization and the prosumer, in Jerónimo, H., Garcia, J., and Mitcham, C. (eds), *Jacques Ellul and the Technological Society in the 21st Century*. Rotterdam: Springer (pp. 35–47).

Robards, B., and Lincoln, S. (2017) Uncovering longitudinal life narratives: scrolling back on Facebook, *Qualitative Research* 17(6): 715–30.

Roberts, S. (2016) Commercial content moderation, in Noble, S., and Tynes, B. (eds), *The Intersectional Internet*. New York: Peter Lang (pp. 147–59).

Robnett, B., and Feliciano, C. (2011) Patterns of racial-ethnic exclusion by internet daters, *Social Forces* 89(3): 807–28.

Rogers, R. (2013) *Digital Methods*. Cambridge, MA: MIT Press.

Rosenblat, A., and Stark, L. (2016) Algorithmic labor and information asymmetries: a case study of Uber's drivers, *International Journal of Communication* 10(27): 3758–84.

Roth, R. (2010) Marx on technical change in the critical edition, *European Journal of Economic Thought* 17(5): 1223–51.

Ruppert, E. (2013) Rethinking empirical social sciences, *Dialogues in Human Geography* 3(3): 268–73.

Ruppert, E., Law, J., and Savage, M. (2013) Reassembling social science methods: the challenge of digital devices, *Theory, Culture and Society* 30(4): 22–46.

Savage, M., and Burrows, R. (2007) The coming crisis of empirical sociology, *Sociology* 41(5): 885–99.

Savage, M., Devine, F., Cunningham, N., Taylor, M., Li, Y., Hjellbrekke, J., ... and Miles, A. (2013) A new model of social class? Findings from the BBC's Great British Class Survey experiment, *Sociology* 47(2): 219–50.

Schneider, C., and Simonetto, D. (2017) Public sociology on Twitter: a space for public pedagogy? *American Sociologist* 48(2): 233–45.

Scholz, T. (2013) Why does digital labor matter now?, in Scholz, T. (ed.), *Digital Labor: The Internet as Playground and Factory*. New York: Routledge (pp. 1–9).

Scholz, T. (2016) *Platform Cooperativism: Challenging the Corporate Sharing Economy*. New York: Rosa Luxemburg Stiftung.

Schor, J., and Attwood-Charles, W. (2017) The "sharing" economy: labor, inequality and sociability on for-profit platforms, *Sociology Compass* 11(8): e12493.

Seaver, N. (2017) Algorithms as culture: some tactics for the ethnography of algorithmic systems, *Big Data & Society* 4(2), http://journals.sagepub.com/doi/pdf/10.1177/2053951717738104.

Selwyn, N. (2016) Teachers vs. technology: rethinking the digitisation of teachers' work, *Professional Voice* 11(2): 18–24.

Selwyn, N., and Pangrazio, L. (2018) Doing data differently? Developing personal data strategies and tactics amongst young social media users, *Big Data & Society* 5(1), https://doi.org/10.1177/2053951718765021.

Selwyn, N., Nemorin, S., and Johnson, N. (2017) High-tech, hard work: an investigation of teachers' work in the digital age, *Learning, Media and Technology* 42(4): 390–405.

Sevignani, S. (2013) *Review of Digital Labor: The Internet as Playground and Factory, tripleC* 11(1): 127–35.

Shahin, S. (2018) Facing up to Facebook, *Information, Communication & Society*, https://doi.org/10.1080/1369118X.2017.1340494.

Shapiro, A. (2018) Between autonomy and control: strategies of arbitrage in the "on-demand" economy, *New Media & Society*, https://doi.org/10.1177/1461444817738236.

Sharma, S. (2013) Black Twitter? Racial hashtags, networks and contagion, *New Formations* 78: 46–64.

Shullenberger, G. (2014) The rise of the voluntariat, *Jacobin*, May 15, www.jacobinmag.com/2014/05/the-rise-of-the-voluntariat/.

Skeggs, B., and Yuill, S. (2016) The methodology of a multi-model project examining how Facebook infrastructures social relations, *Information, Communication & Society* 19(10): 1356–72.

Smit, R., Ansgard, H., and Broersma, M. (2017) Activating the past in the Ferguson protests: memory work, digital activism and the politics of platforms, *New Media & Society*, https://doi.org/10.1177/1461444817741849.

Srnicek, N. (2017) *Platform Capitalism*. Cambridge: Polity.

Stanworth, M. (1987) *Reproductive Technologies: Gender, Motherhood and Medicine*. Minneapolis: University of Minnesota Press.

Star, S. (1999) The ethnography of infrastructure, *American Behavioral Scientist* 43(3): 377–91.

Statistica (2018) Most popular social networks worldwide as of April 2018, ranked by number of active users, www.statista.com/statistics/272014/global-social-networks-ranked-by-number-of-users/.

Stein, J. (2016) Tyranny of the mob, *Time* 188(8): 26–32.

Sterne, J. (2003) Bourdieu, technique and technology, *Cultural Studies* 17(3/4): 367–89.

Stewart, B. (2016) Collapsed publics: orality, literacy, and vulnerability in academic Twitter, *Journal of Applied Social Theory* 1(1), http://socialtheoryapplied.com/journal/jast/article/view/33/9.

Taffel, S. (2016) Perspectives on the postdigital, *Convergence* 22(3): 324–38.

Takahashi, T. (2014) Youth, social media and connectivity in Japan, in Seargeant, P., and Tagg, C. (eds), *The Language of Social Media*. Basingstoke: Palgrave Macmillan (pp. 186–207).

Tanksley, T. (2016) Education, representation and resistance, in Noble, S., and Tynes, B. (eds), *The Intersectional Internet*. New York: Peter Lang (pp. 243–59).

Terranova, T. (2000) Free labor: producing culture for the digital economy, *Social Text* 18(2): 33–58.

Thebault-Spieker, J., Terveen, L., and Hecht, B. (2015) Avoiding the south side and the suburbs: the geography of mobile crowdsourcing markets, in *Proceedings of the 18th ACM Conference on Computer Supported Cooperative Work and Social Computing*. New York: ACM (pp. 265–75).

Turkle, S. (1995) *Life on the Screen: Identity in the Age of the Internet*. New York: Simon & Schuster.

Turner, F. (2017) Don't be evil: Fred Turner on utopias, frontiers, and brogrammers, *Logic* no. 3, https://logicmag.io/03-dont-be-evil/.

Valluvan, S. (2016) What is "post-race" and what does it reveal about contemporary racisms? *Ethnic and Racial Studies* 39(13): 2241–51.

van Dijck, J., Poell, T., and de Waal, M. (2018) *The Platform Society: Public Values for a Connective World / De platformsamenleving:*

strijd om publieke waarden in een online wereld. Oxford: Oxford University Press.

van Zoonen, L. (1992) Feminist theory and information technology, *Media, Culture and Society* 14(1): 9–29.

Veblen, T. (1904) *The Theory of Business Enterprise.* New Brunswick, NJ: Transaction Books.

Veletsianos, G., and Kimmons, R. (2012) Assumptions and challenges of open scholarship, *International Review of Research in Open and Distributed Learning* 13(4): 166–89.

Venturini, T., and Latour, B. (2010) The social fabric: digital traces and quali-quantitative methods, *Proceedings of Futur en Seine 2009: The Digital Future of the City.* Paris: Cap Digital (pp. 87–101).

Venturini, T., Jacomy, M., Meunier, A., and Latour, B. (2017) An unexpected journey: a few lessons from sciences Po médialab's experience, *Big Data & Society* 4(2), https://doi.org/10.1177/2053951717720949.

Volti, R. (2004) William F. Ogburn, social change with respect to culture and original nature, *Technology and Culture* 45: 396–405.

Wajcman, J. (2009) Feminist theories of technology, *Cambridge Journal of Economics* 34(1): 143–52.

Walker, A. (2012) Labor of recombination, *Subjectivity: International Journal of Critical Psychology* 5(1): 36–53.

Wang, T. (2013) Why Big Data needs thick data, *Ethnography Matters*, May 13, https://medium.com/ethnography-matters/why-big-data-needs-thick-data-b4b3e75e3d7.

Wark, M. (2016) The stack to come, *Public Seminar*, December 28, www.publicseminar.org/2016/12/stack/.

Wark, M. (2017) *General Intellects: Twenty-Five Thinkers for the Twenty-First Century.* London: Verso.

Webster, A. (2013) Afterword: digital technology and social windows, in Orton-Johnson, K., and Prior, N. (ed.), *Digital Sociology: Critical Perspectives.* Basingstoke: Palgrave Macmillan (pp. 227–33).

Weinstein, J. (1982) *Sociology/Technology.* New Brunswick, NJ: Transaction Books.

Weller, M. (2011) *The Digital Scholar: How Technology is Transforming Scholarly Practice.* London: Continuum.

Wellman, B. (2004) The three ages of internet studies: ten, five and zero years ago, *New Media Society* 6: 123–9.

Weltevrede, E. J. T. (2016) *Repurposing Digital Methods: The Research Affordances of Platforms and Engines.* Doctoral dissertation, University of Amsterdam, http://dare.uva.nl/document/2/168511.

Weltevrede, E., and Borra, E. (2016) Platform affordances and data practices: the value of dispute on Wikipedia, *Big Data & Society* 3(1), https://doi.org/10.1177/2053951716653418.

Wilkie, A., Michael, M., and Plummer-Fernandez, M. (2015) Speculative method and Twitter: bots, energy and three conceptual characters, *Sociological Review* 63(1): 79–101.

Williams, A. (2016) On Thursdays we watch *Scandal*: communal viewing and Black Twitter, in Daniels, J., Cottom, T., and Gregory, K. (eds), *Digital Sociologies*. Bristol: Policy Press (pp. 273–91).

Williams, M., and Burnap, P. (2015) Cyberhate on social media in the aftermath of Woolwich: a case study in computational criminology and Big Data, *British Journal of Criminology* 56(2): 211–38.

Williams, M., Burnap, P., and Sloan, L. (2017) Crime sensing with Big Data: the affordances and limitations of using open-source communications to estimate crime patterns, *British Journal of Criminology* 57(2): 320–40.

Willis, E. (1996) *The Sociological Quest: An Introduction to the Study of Social Life*. New Brunswick, NJ: Rutgers University Press.

Winner, L. (1986) Do artefacts have politics?, in Winner, *The Whale and the Reactor*. Chicago: University of Chicago Press (pp. 19–39).

Winner, L. (1993) Upon opening the black box and finding it empty: social constructivism and the philosophy of technology, *Science, Technology and Human Values* 18(3): 362–78.

Woodcock, J. (2018) Digital labour in the university: understanding the transformations of academic work in the UK, *tripleC* 16(1): 114–28.

Woolgar, S. (1991) The turn to technology in social studies of science, *Science, Technology and Human Values* 16(1): 20–50.

Zook, M., Barocas, S., Boyd, D., Crawford, K., Keller, E., and Gangadharan, S. (2017) Ten simple rules for responsible Big Data research, *PLoS Computational Biology* 13(3):e1005399.

Index

Academic Twitter 95–6, 109–10
affect 20, 41, 105, 108
agency 12, 44, 57, 59
Airbnb 27, 28, 61
algorithm 5, 25, 29–31, 43, 51, 52, 62, 69, 72–3, 75, 77, 83, 86, 88, 108
Amazon 27, 54, 110
Amazon Mechanical Turk viii, 50–2, 58
Apple 4, 27
automation 7, 29–31, 48, 49, 50, 52, 55, 63, 73, 77, 85, 110

Bauman, Zygmunt 32–4
Bell, Daniel 15, 18
Big Data 15, 29, 73–9, 82, 86, 88–90, 104, 112
Black Lives Matter 64, 67
blogging 21, 48, 54, 65, 97

capitalism 5, 7, 15, 18, 28, 35, 36, 55, 69
Castells, Manuel 15, 19, 26, 35
Chun, Wendy 26, 41, 42, 44
code(d) 4, 20, 24, 43, 51, 67, 80, 83, 84, 85, 86, 100, 110

coding 21, 62, 82–6, 88, 91, 101
commodification 35, 53, 61
community 16, 25, 26, 64–5, 80, 81, 109
computational social sciences 73–9, 86, 90
computer science 16, 42, 75, 88, 100
control 15, 17, 25, 30, 31, 36–9, 41, 50–2, 56, 66, 78, 107, 111
cooperative 54, 69, 101, 104
Cottom, Tressie 59, 66

Daniels, Jessie 58, 60, 61, 66
data 4, 5, 15, 18, 20, 25, 28–31, 35, 36, 38–40, 48–53, 62, 71–91, 93, 96, 100, 101, 103, 104, 107, 110, 112
data science 75, 88, 89, 93
dataveillance 18, 104
Deleuze, Gilles 38–40
deskilling 49, 50
digital humanities 43, 101, 112
digital labor 37, 45–58, 104, 105
digital scholarship 92, 100, 105, 106, 108, 109, 110, 112

Ellul, Jacques 10, 18, 19
ethics 10, 62, 100
ethnography 69, 78, 80–2, 90
exclusion 46, 52

Facebook 3, 4, 17, 28, 36, 37,
 39, 40, 44, 53, 56, 62, 63, 65,
 66, 67, 75, 83, 84, 86, 88, 89
feminist perspectives on
 technology 14, 18, 19, 37,
 69
Foucault, Michel 37–8, 40, 41,
 44
free labour 53–4

Galloway, Alexander 39, 41,
 42, 44
gender 14, 15, 34, 46, 53, 55,
 59, 104
gig economy/work 36, 50, 51,
 55, 56, 58, 104
Google 3, 4, 17, 27, 28, 31,
 37, 62, 67, 84, 97, 98, 108

hashtag 64, 79, 84, 93, 95
human 9, 10, 14, 18, 24, 28,
 30, 32, 33, 37, 39, 41, 42, 43,
 57, 63, 73, 74, 82–4, 86, 110

identity 14, 16, 18, 19, 26, 31,
 63–4, 70
inequality 16, 18, 27, 40, 44,
 48, 55, 58, 59, 60, 62, 68,
 110
infrastructure 27, 37, 43, 51,
 53, 80
innovation 6, 8, 18, 31, 71
Instagram 55, 63, 76
interdisciplinary 2, 11, 75, 89,
 90–3, 95, 99, 108, 111
Internet of Things 4, 19
internet studies 16, 18
intersectionality 19, 60

journalism 27, 48, 50, 56

live methods 72, 83, 85

Marres, Noortje 73, 74, 77, 83,
 87, 88, 100
Marx/Marxian theory 7, 8, 17,
 18, 20, 25, 33, 35–7, 40, 45,
 104
metrics 49, 56, 62, 107, 108
micro-celebrity 55, 108
Mumford, Lewis 9, 18

network 2, 3, 4, 9, 15, 17, 19,
 22, 25–7, 31, 36, 38–41, 50,
 65, 66, 69, 75, 76, 80, 86,
 94–5, 110, 112

open access 98, 106

panoptic 38, 39, 62
pedagogy 86, 94, 99–100
platform 3, 18, 19, 20, 24, 25,
 27–8, 31, 36, 37, 43, 51–3,
 55, 61–3, 64, 65, 67–9, 76,
 77, 79, 83, 84, 86, 95, 96,
 104, 105, 108, 110, 117
political economy 18, 25, 36,
 44
post-digital 23–4, 113
public sociology 20, 102–4

race 19, 34, 45, 46, 52, 57–70,
 77
racism 58, 61–2, 67, 68, 77
Rogers, Richard 83, 87

Scholz, Trebor 57, 69, 104
search 3, 27, 30, 31, 98, 108
smartphone 3, 4, 23, 57, 85
social media 3, 4, 16, 36, 40,
 53–7, 63, 64, 67, 72, 74, 76,
 79, 81, 84, 93, 95, 96, 102,
 103, 107, 108, 109, 110
social theory *see* theory (social)
software studies 83, 88
structure (social) 25, 33, 43,
 44, 57, 60, 111
STS (science and technology
 studies) 11–13, 18, 19, 80
surveillance 28, 37–39, 52, 81

teaching   49, 85, 94, 99–100,
    105, 106
theory (social)   2, 5–17, 23, 26,
    34–40, 40–4, 69, 74, 111, 114
thick data   78–80, 86, 112
trace   79, 80, 86
Twitter   61, 63–8, 76–9, 84, 85,
    87, 89, 95–7, 102, 103, 105,
    106, 109, 110

Uber   24, 25, 27, 28, 51–3, 55,
    56, 58, 69, 110

Weber, Max   6, 17, 19
Wikipedia   3, 80, 97
Winner, Langdon   12, 18

YouTube   3, 36, 54, 55, 63,
    65